Managing Facilities Management

IT Infrastructure Library

Central Computer and
Telecommunications Agency
Gildengate House, Upper Green Lane
Norwich NR3 1DW

This is one of the first books to be published in
the IT Infrastructure Library series. At regular
intervals, further books will be published and the
Library will be completed by late 1991. Since
many customers would like to receive the IT
Infrastructure Library books automatically on
publication, a standing order service has been set
up. For further details on standing orders please
contact:

HMSO Publicity(P9D), FREEPOST,
Norwich, NR3 1BR
(*No stamp needed for UK customers*).

Until the whole Library is published, and subject
to availability, draft copies of unpublished books
may be obtained from CCTA if you are a
standing order customer. To obtain drafts please
contact:

IT Infrastructure Management Services, CCTA,
Gildengate House, Upper Green Lane, Norwich
NR3 1DW.

For further information on other CCTA
products, contact

Press and Public Relations,
CCTA
Riverwalk House
157-161 Millbank
London SW1P 4RT.

This document has been produced using
procedures conforming to
BSI 5750 Part 1: 1987; ISO 9001: 1987.

Table of Contents

Foreword

Welcome to the IT Infrastructure Library
Managing Facilities Management *module.*

In their respective subject areas, the IT Infrastructure Library publications complement and provide more detail than the IS Guides.

The ethos behind the development of the IT Infrastructure Library is the recognition that organizations are becoming increasingly dependent on IT in order to satisfy their corporate aims and meet their business needs. This growing dependency leads to a growing requirement for high-quality IT services. In this context quality means matched to business needs and user requirements as these evolve.

This module is one of a series of codes of practice intended to facilitate the quality management of IT Services, and of the IT Infrastructure. (By IT Infrastructure, we mean organizations' computers and networks - hardware, software and computer-related telecommunications, upon which applications systems and IT services are built and run). The codes of practice are intended to assist organizations to provide quality IT service in the face of skill shortages, system complexity, rapid change, current and future user requirements, growing user expectations, etc.

Underpinning the IT Infrastructure is the Environmental Infrastructure upon which it is built. Environmental topics are covered in a separate set of guides within the IT Infrastructure Library.

IT Infrastructure Management is a complex subject which for presentational and practical reasons has been broken down within the IT Infrastructure Library into a series of modules. A complete list of current and planned modules is available from the CCTA IT Infrastructure Management Services at the address given at the back of this module.

The structure of this module is in essence :

* *a Management Summary aimed at senior managers (Directors of IT and above, senior IT people and in some cases "senior customers" (typically Civil Service grades 3 - 7)*

* *the main body of the text aimed at IT middle management (typically grades 7 to HEO)*

* *technical detail in Annexes.*

*The module gives the main **guidance** in Sections 3 to 5; explains the **benefits, costs and possible problems** in Section 6, which may be of interest to senior staff; and provides information on **tools** (requirements and examples of real-life availability) in Section 7.*

CCTA is working with the IT industry to foster the development of software tools to underpin the guidance contained within the codes of practice (ie to make adherence to the module more practicable), and ultimately to automate functions.

If you have any comments on this or other modules, do please let us know. A comment sheet is provided with every module; please feel free to photocopy the comment sheet or to let us have your views via any other medium.

Thank you. We hope you find this module useful.

1. Management Summary

1.1 Background

Organizations are becoming increasingly dependent on their IT services. This means they require quality IT services. But many organizations are facing difficulties in recruiting and retaining the necessary skilled staff. Facilities Management (FM) can lessen these problems.

Organizations using an FM provider continue to be responsible for the running of their business. To have confidence that the quality of their IT services - upon which the running of their business depends - will be maintained, it is essential that they effectively manage their relationship with the FM provider.

1.2 Outline of Module

This module of the IT Infrastructure Library complements the CCTA IS Guide on Facilities Management. The IS Guide gives advice to organizations that are considering the use of a Facilities Management (FM) arrangement for the provision of IT services. The Guide explains how organizations should position themselves to take full advantage of FM, and outlines the processes that need to be followed to ensure both a successful FM planning/implementation project and the satisfactory operation, management and control of IT services using FM.

This module gives detailed guidance on the plans and controls required by an organization to manage its ongoing relationship with an FM provider (whether a private sector contractor or another government organization).

The term Facilities Management (FM) is generic and refers to a variety of activities and functions. For the purposes of this module FM is defined as the management and operation of part, or all, of an organization's IT services by an external source:

* at agreed service levels

* to an agreed cost formula

* over an agreed period.

The provision of technical IT advice to the organization may also be included in an FM contract.

FM can involve the assumption of control over some or all of an organization's existing IT infrastructure management activities and IT services by a third party. FM can also involve the provision of a completely new service, and perhaps development of the software to run on such a service. FM can, but need not, involve ownership of hardware and software by the FM provider - though in general the FM provider is likely to be responsible for the administration of contracts for the supply and maintenance of hardware and software. The use of a bureau service can also be regarded as a type of FM.

This module concentrates primarily on the takeover by an FM provider of an existing operation - either from an organization's own staff or from a previous FM provider. Most of the guidance is however equally applicable to, or can be easily generalized to cover, greenfield situations and the other types of FM just described.

1.3 Relationship with FM Provider

It is in an organization's best interest that the company providing its FM is business-like and profit-making. This means, however, that the more demanding the requirement (eg faster transaction response times, sole use of hardware etc), the greater the cost is likely to be. It is therefore essential that organizations' IT service requests are set in accordance with the needs of their businesses.

To ensure organizations get an IT service of the quality needed to support the operation of their business it is vital that they formalize and manage their relationship with the FM provider in accordance with the following principles:

*   specify and agree end user service requirements in the form of Service Level Agreements (SLAs)

*   ensure that the requirements in the SLAs are reflected appropriately in the provisions of the FM contract

*   monitor the quality of provided service (the 'service levels') and ensure remedial action is taken if it is not up to the standards specified in the SLAs

*   understand and audit the processes used to provide the service.

Users of CCTA's procurement service can have the standard CCTA General Conditions of Contract (CC88) adapted to incorporate service level criteria, which reflect the requirements set out in individual SLAs and form the basis for monitoring the service provided against the contract. CCTA recommends that any contract for the provision of FM includes the requirement to provide quality IT services using specific parts of, or specific principles extracted from, the IT Infrastructure Library.

If the service level criteria are not met, or the agreed procedures are not fully used, it is the customer organization's responsibility to:

* agree a remedial plan with the FM provider

* invoke contractual financial remedies if necessary.

Organizations must realize that FM is not a panacea to remove all their IT worries. They will still have a requirement for high level IT management skills. Organizations that pass their IT service provision to an external body should therefore pay particular attention to developing and maintaining IT management skills in house.

1.4 Need for Service Control Team

CCTA recommends that any organization using an FM provider maintains an IT presence in the form of a Service Control Team (SCT). The SCT is responsible for the technical management of the FM contract, for overseeing the provision of IT services from the customers' side and for auditing the processes used by the FM provider. For organizations that require their FM provider to use the IT Infrastructure Library, checklists for auditing the FM provider's processes are available in section 5 of the relevant IT Infrastructure Library modules.

1.5 Staffing Issues

When a decision is made to use an FM provider, internal staffing issues should be handled sensitively and reasonably. Where the FM provider takes over an existing service, the organization's staff are often offered employment with the FM provider. It is important to work for positive staff reaction.

1.6 Confidence

The takeover of an existing operation by a new FM provider does not guarantee significantly better quality or cheaper services. However, if organizations follow the advice given in this module they can have reasonable confidence that quality IT services will be provided.

2. Introduction

FM is concerned with the provision of IT services and the running of IT infrastructure management activities by a third party. Application software and development may or may not be included. The IT systems upon which the services are run may or may not be located on the user organization's premises, and these systems may be owned by the organization or by the FM provider. A computer bureau also provides a form of FM service.

This module concentrates on the takeover by an FM provider of an existing IT operation either from an organization's own staff of from a previous FM provider. However the advice can easily be generalized to apply to other types of FM. The module does not attempt to cover the provision of application development by a third party, but it does cover the implications for applications development of transferring IT infrastructure management to an FM provider.

Interest in FM is growing. This interest can be attributed, at least in part, to the considerable problems encountered by IT service providers eg:

*   the difficulty of attracting and retaining staff of the required calibre

*   the need for quality IT services, stemming from a growing dependency on IT

*   increasing and unpredictable demands on the IT services

*   moves toward decentralization of IT

*   cash constraints.

The difficulty organizations are having in coping with these problems is highlighted in part by the growing use of consultancy services. The use of FM is, in a sense, a logical next step.

In the public sector there is in addition a trend towards privatizing certain services. Some local government, central government and NHS authorities have already put out their internal IT service provision to competitive tender and legislation already exists to enable ministers to require local authorities to do this.

It is pertinent for all organizations, particularly Civil Service ones, to consider how they would cope if they entrusted their IT services to an FM provider.

It is important to note from the outset that ultimate responsibility for the IT service on which the organization's business objectives depend cannot be devolved to an FM provider. This must, and will, remain with the organization's management.

Note that the term organization is used throughout this module to refer to an organization that uses an FM provider - ie a customer organization such as a government department or agency.

2.1 Purpose

The purpose of this module is to provide guidance to organizations on how to manage their relationship with an FM provider. FM cannot reliably be left to look after itself. This module gives guidance on the plans and controls required to manage an FM contract.

2.2 Target Readership

This module is aimed at Members of IS Steering Committees, IT Executive Committees and IS Planning Secretariats; Directors of IT; IT Services Managers; Service Control Team(SCT) Managers; User/Business Managers; Facilities Management providers and Procurement Officers. For further information on SCT Managers please refer to section 3.1.2.

2.3 Scope

This module covers both technical and administrative considerations for the management of FM. (The guidance does not explicitly cover greenfield sites but other than where the transfer of existing services to a new FM provider is being discussed, the advice is applicable.)

The main considerations are:

* underpinning individual Service Level Agreements (SLAs) - see 3.1.4.1 - by including in the FM contract an adaptation of CC88 to include service level criteria; specifically, an appendix to CC88 part 2-C can be used suitably modified for the purpose

* monitoring for adherence to contract

* plans and controls to be used by the FM provider (service levels, capacity, availability, contingency, change, problem management etc)

* rights of inspection to audit for compliance with plans and controls

* actions to be taken if SLA requirements are not achieved or agreed procedures not fully used

* change control between organization and FM provider

* IT standards

* staff

* ownership of hardware and software

* location of hardware

* security

* duration of contract

* designated handover procedures (to ensure a smooth transfer of work when changing from one IT provider to another).

This module briefly addresses the cultural changes associated with contracting out IT service provision, and the steps (technical and contractual) organizations must take to guard against being locked into one FM provider.

Private sector experience is that, at the end of an FM contract, organizations either renew their current FM contract or change to a new FM provider. It is important to note that few outside organizations attempt to rebuild their IT expertise, and it is unlikely that any government department could do so, once it was committed to the use of FM. A possible exception is if a large organization transferred a small part of its IT services, or a small aspect of its IT service provision, to FM. This module gives brief guidance to organizations to ensure that they can change FM provider, or stop using FM if they can recreate IT expertise internally, if they wish.

This module covers the supply by FM providers of a total IT service, and of the totality of IT infrastructure management functions. By implication, it covers individual parts of the service and individual functions. Figure 1 shows the organizational placement, and a selection of the responsibilities, of an internally-provided IT services section. Figure 2 shows how the organizational structure changes when IT services responsibilities are handed over to FM.

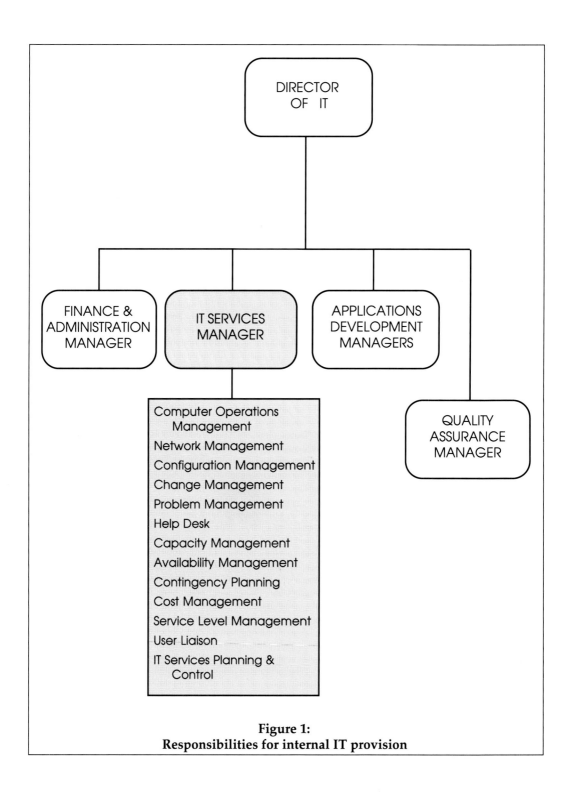

Figure 1:
Responsibilities for internal IT provision

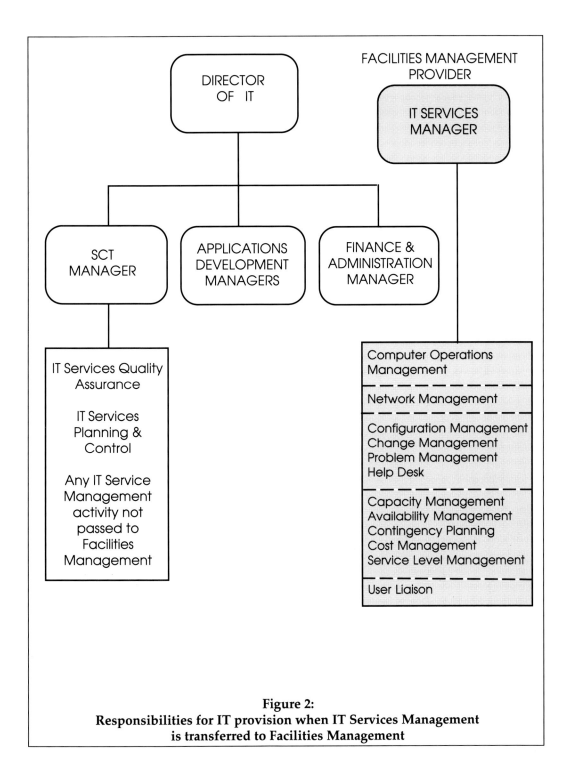

Figure 2:
Responsibilities for IT provision when IT Services Management
is transferred to Facilities Management

FM can be provided for some or all of the IT infrastructure management activities covered by the IT Infrastructure Library - a selection of which is shown under IT Services Manager in figures 1 and 2. If only some of the functions shown in these figures are to be transferred, these are likely to be in a contiguous block, starting from the top of the shaded list downwards. This is because, broadly, the functions towards the bottom of the list are dependent for their successful operation on those shown above them. For example, it would be unusual for an FM provider to take on Service Level Management (SLM) without having control of supporting processes shown above it in the figure. Natural blocks of functions to be transferred are demarcated in figure 2 by dotted lines.

CCTA recommends that organizations keep responsibility for quality audit and planning and control (see figure 2). Applications software maintenance can be included in the responsibility of the FM provider. Applications development may be provided internally by the organization, by a software house, or by an FM company. Advice on how to manage applications development is outside the scope of the IT Infrastructure Library. However, the module briefly addresses the implications for managing FM of adopting each of these options.

The guidance contained in this module is appropriate to all kinds of FM, including short term FM to handle the run down of old equipment.

Note that this module does not cover how to decide between in-house IT service provision and an FM provided IT service. Please see the CCTA IS Guide on Facilities Management for further details.

2.4 Related guidance

This book is one of a series of modules issued as part of the CCTA IT Infrastructure Library. Although this module can be read in isolation, it should be used in conjunction with other IT Infrastructure Library modules.

All the IT Infrastructure Library modules are highly relevant as CCTA recommends the use of the practices and procedures described in the IT Infrastructure Library, for FM contracts. The **Service Level Management** module is particularly important as it provides guidance to organizations on how to frame their service level requirements with the FM provider, and on the ongoing maintenance and management of the SLAs that form a basis of their contract with the FM provider.

It is believed that FM providers will accept the IT Infrastructure Library as a code of practice for managing the services provided, as it documents the good practices they should be using anyway.

2.5 Standards

ISO 9001 / EN2900 / BS5750 - Quality Management and Quality Assurance Standards

The IT Infrastructure Library modules are being designed to assist adherents to obtain third-party quality certification to ISO 9001. CCTA recommends that FM providers are required to use the principles set out in the IT Infrastructure Library modules and that the FM provider's IT infrastructure/service management procedures are certified by a third party certification body to ISO 9001. Such third parties should be accredited by the NACCB, the National Accreditation Council for Certification Bodies.

Other standards

The organization should stipulate any other IT standard it requires the FM provider to adhere to (eg GOSIP).

FM providers should table their standards and procedures as part of the procurement process. The organization should know how the FM provider proposes to work. Any FM providers proposing not to adhere to the IT Infrastructure Library codes of practice must detail how they will satisfy organizations' requirements using different procedures.

3. Planning for Managing FM

This section gives guidance on the plans required to give confidence that a quality IT service, to support the running of an organization's business, will be maintained when using an FM provider.

3.1 Procedures

Once it is decided to move to FM, the organization must decide what is required in sufficient outline to tell potential FM providers and to arrive at approximate costings:

* decide the work/IT services to be run under FM

* decide the IT infrastructure management activities (and any others appropriate eg applications development) to be transferred to the FM provider

* set up and define the role of the Service Control Team (SCT) - see 3.1.2

* draw up the implementation plan

* plan how FM will be managed

* set up service quality and other measures against which to judge the FM provider's services

* draw up plans to facilitate handover to another FM provider, if necessary, at the end of the contract.

Based on the work just described, the next priorities are to:

* draw up a Statement of Service Requirements(SSR) to tell potential FM providers what is required (the requirements being refined at contract drafting stage if necessary) - where the FM provider is contracting to run new applications SSADM techniques can be used

* invite proposals by competitive tender

* discuss and reach agreement with shortlisted bidders

* evaluate tenders

* place the contract

* implement FM.

Execution of the guidance in sections 3 and 4 of this module on planning and implementing FM should be carried out as a project using the PRINCE method. The project deliverable will be the implemented FM service. The PRINCE management organization should consist of a:

* project board chair

* senior user member

* senior IT member (normally from the FM provider)

* business assurance coordinator (probably from the SCT)

* user assurance coordinator (from the user/customer community)

* technical assurance coordinator (from the SCT)

* Project/Stage Managers.

The project board may also wish to co-opt onto the project staff with responsibility for, and expertise in, such matters as finance and contracting.

Further information on project management can be found in PRINCE documentation, which is available from CCTA, and from CCTA IS Guide A5 on Project Management.

3.1.1 Plan Work, Services and Functions to be run by the FM provider

The process of deciding whether or not to go to FM will have broadly outlined the scope of the activities to be passed to FM. Further detailed work may now be required.

Organizations must decide:

* what work and IT services are to be run by the FM provider

* which of the functions covered by IT Infrastructure Library modules are to be supplied by the FM provider.

Guidance on the work or services to consider for running by the FM provider is available in the CCTA IS Guide E4 on FM. In general, these services should correspond to whole management domains, to avoid problems of split responsibility. For example, it would be inadvisable to transfer some but not all of the services running concurrently on a single computer system.

Figure 1 (page 8) shows selected functions that are generally the responsibilities of an organization's IT Services Section that may be put out to FM. As previously stated in 2.3, there are natural blocks of functions in a hierarchy which could be passed to FM - see, for example, figure 2 (page 9).

If a decision has been made not to contract out certain functions to FM, define formal interfaces between those functions contracted out and the ones kept in-house. See the appropriate IT Infrastructure Library modules for more details on these interfaces.

3.1.2 Plan and set up the Service Control Team (SCT)

To manage the organization's side of the relationship with the FM provider, the organization should set up an SCT which must retain a level of expertise in IT. The SCT should be headed by one of the organization's senior IT Managers - probably the person who would have been IT Services Manager if IT infrastructure management was being done by an in-house team. The SCT Manager is the organization's normal interface with the FM provider, and is responsible during planning and implementation of FM to the FM project board. The size of the SCT obviously varies dependent on the size and complexity of service being provided by the FM company, but a reasonable estimate would be for the SCT to be approximately 5% of the size of the service provider, in staffing terms. The skill levels required of SCT members would equate approximately to those of an IT business analyst.

The SCT is responsible for:

* carrying out the planning activities described in 3.1 and overseeing the implementation of FM, both under the control of the project board

* overseeing the ongoing management of FM

    - monitoring quality measures (IT service quality, FM provider's outputs/management reports)

    - quality auditing of processes

    - acting as the main interface to the FM provider on all service-related matters (other than where direct user-FM liaison is appropriate)

    - controlling activities not handed over to FM

* overseeing the handover at the end of the contract.

These activities are covered in more detail later in this module. Other possible SCT functions and activities which are not covered in detail include:

* provision of unbiased strategic IT advice to the organization

* managing IT services activities not handed over to FM

* overall control of technical planning

* business analysis regarding new applications systems and project management for the development and introduction of new applications systems

* support for users' business queries

* end-user training - a good FM provider is not necessarily a good training provider

* acting as a nucleus to help rebuild internal IT provision if it became necessary. It must be remembered however that this course of action could be taken by many organizations only in exceptional circumstances, due to difficulties in attracting IT staff.

Organizations should normally retain control, through the SCT, over the decisions relating to the introduction of new services, the evaluation of proposals for new services and the enhancement of existing services. However, the FM provider has an input to the organization's decision making processes, particularly when the new service or enhancement is to be included in the FM contract.

The SCT occupies a pivotal role in the relationship between the business and the FM provider. In broad terms the relationship between the users, IT Services/FM providers and IT infrastructure suppliers/maintainers is the same as when a service is being provided internally - see figure 3. For FM, these relationships must be formalized with defined responsibilities and interfaces.

The FM provider is responsible for delivering quality IT services, as specified in SLAs and formalized contractually, to the organization's users. It is usual for the FM provider to administer contracts with IT infrastructure suppliers and maintainers in support of these IT services.

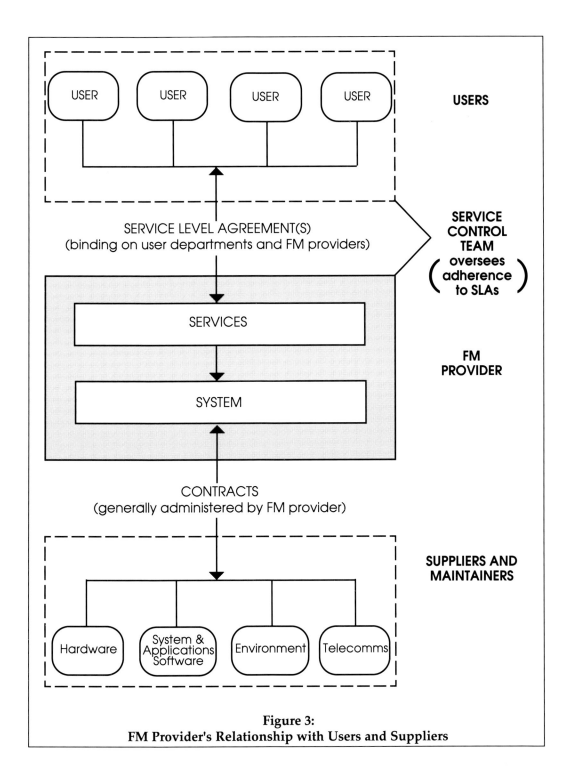

**Figure 3:
FM Provider's Relationship with Users and Suppliers**

The SCT is responsible for the technical management of the organization's contract with the FM provider. This responsibility includes:

* monitoring the quality of delivered service

* auditing the FM provider's activities for compliance to agreed procedures and standards

* liaising with the FM provider

* generally looking after the users' interests with the FM provider and overseeing the smooth running of SLAs on the users' behalf.

The functions just described ensure that, although day to day management of the IT services is passed over to the FM provider, overall control remains with the organization.

To enable the SCT to carry out this role it must be stated in the contract with the FM provider that the SCT has access, according to predefined rules, to all appropriate sites and procedures.

3.1.3 Plan Start-up Activities

Plan for the FM provider to supply key personnel to cover start-up activities (see 4.1.1 for more details). These key personnel should be on site 30 to 90 days prior to transfer and must have fully documented plans to take on:

* technical functions (see 3.1.4 and 4.1)

* personnel (see 3.3)

and, outside the scope of this module,

* financial and administrative functions (eg payroll, paying licences, buying software and hardware).

The organization should check that these plans exist and should satisfy itself that they are adequate. It is the SCT's responsibility to check that the plan for handing over technical functions is adequate. Acceptance testing of the FM service must be planned (see 4.1.1). It is vital that during start-up adequate backout plans are in place to ensure the continued availability of service if the start-up phase is not successfully completed. See 4.1.3 for more details.

Figure 4 shows the relationship between a new provider's start-up and an existing provider's hand-over. See 3.1.5 for guidance on planning the hand-over.

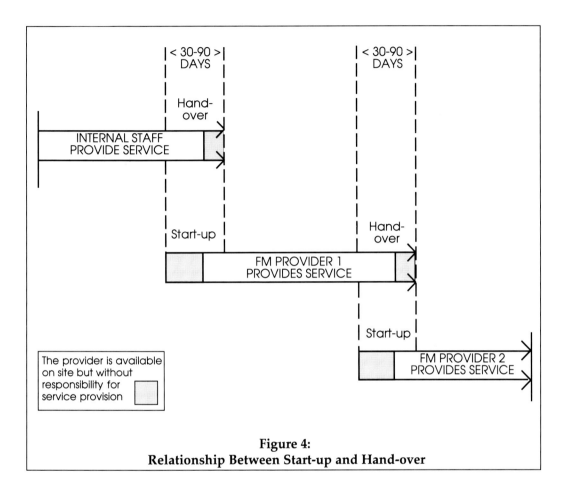

Figure 4:
Relationship Between Start-up and Hand-over

3.1.4 Plan the Ongoing Management of FM

Plans must be made for the ongoing management of the organization's relationship with the FM provider. The purpose of this ongoing management is to ensure the required quality IT service is provided. In principle, there is no difference in controlling the quality of service whether it is being provided internally or by FM provider. In either case there must be agreed and documented:

* a specification of service quality requirements

* a mechanism for updating this specification to ensure it continues to reflect customer requirements

* a set of systematic and auditable processes for delivering the services

* a way of monitoring that the required service quality is being delivered

* a mechanism for correcting deficiencies.

However, the responsibilities are different. For an internally-provided service the organization's IT Directorate is responsible for providing and monitoring the service, auditing the processes and putting right deficiencies. In other words the IT Directorate must supply a quality service and ensure that this is done (line management controls apply). For FM, it is the FM provider's responsibility to provide the required quality service. The organization must ensure that this is done.

The FM provider must supply the service according to IT Infrastructure Library principles and practices, centred on Service Level Agreements and Service Level Management, or a demonstrable equivalent. This gives confidence that a quality service will be maintained. Use by FM providers of IT Infrastructure Library principles and practices allows organizations to compare like with like when evaluating tenders, and aids the transition between one FM provider and another, if so required, thus reducing the likelihood of the organization becoming locked into one provider.

The quality audit function, which independently monitors the FM provider's services and audits the FM provider's processes, should not be run by the FM provider itself. It is recommended that the quality audit function is the responsibility of the SCT. Some aspects of quality are not easily quantifiable (eg the telephone manner of the Help Desk) but these too need to be audited and monitored by the SCT (probably based on feedback from the users) and dealt with at regular review meetings. The SCT must have access to all customer complaints, and must have the right to arbitrate on behalf of the organization's management, when disputes between the user and the FM provider cannot be resolved.

3.1.4.1 Service Level Agreements (SLAs)

The full range of services to be supplied, and functions to be carried out, by the FM provider is specified in a Statement of Service Requirement (SSR) - see 3.1.6.1. The management responsibilities of the FM provider are included. The FM provider's most important responsibility is to provide quality IT which is specified in quantitative terms in the form of Service Level Requirements (SLRs). Once the SLRs have been agreed in the contract they become SLAs. The method by which IT services are provided is not usually included in the SLAs but is specified in the contract.

The main basis for managing an FM contract is the SLA. SLAs detail the organization's requirements for IT service quality (service levels) including factors such as service levels, availability, reliability, security, adherence to required functionality, user support levels, capacity for growth and any changed service levels when a contingency plan has to be invoked.

SLAs are the criteria against which the provided service is monitored.

SLAs should include target performance figures for the FM provider's IT services eg 95% of terminal response times for enquiry transactions to be less than 1 second. The SLAs should also contain restrictions on the volumes and types of transactions for the user eg a maximum of 15,000 enquiry transactions per hour. If it comes to light (eg via service review meetings - see 3.1.4.3) that the FM provider's targets will not be met, changes should be instigated to maintain the agreed service levels. These changes could involve:

* provision of extra capacity (may be chargeable if the hardware is owned by the FM provider, unless the FM provider is at fault and the contract stipulates that, in these circumstances, the extra capacity must be provided at the FM provider's expense)

* reductions to the agreed service levels (likely to be unpopular with users especially if the FM provider is at fault, and to reduce user productivity)

* some form of demand management, to limit the use of IT resources (can be used as a temporary measure).

Further information is available in the IT Infrastructure Library **Capacity Management** module.

It is important to realize that SLAs impose a discipline on the organization as well as the FM provider. If the users do not adhere to the limits agreed by them in the SLA, the FM provider cannot be held responsible for not providing the agreed service levels.

Annex C gives a skeleton SLA which organizations can use as a model for their own. More information on Service Level Management, including SLAs, is available in the IT Infrastructure Library **Service Level Management** module.

The Service Level Manager, who is generally a member of the FM provider's staff, is responsible for the quality of service provided to the users. It is therefore the FM provider's responsibility to manage the service and ensure there is adequate support by suppliers and maintainers to underpin the SLAs.

3.1.4.2 Management Reports

Once an FM provider has taken over responsibility for running an organization's services and functions this provider is required to provide regular detailed management reports.

The type and general contents of reports must be agreed between the organization and the FM provider at the planning stage to ensure that the FM provider is later capable of producing the required information. Details of what should be reported are given at 5.1.1.

3.1.4.3 Service Review Meetings

As part of the ongoing management of FM regular service review meetings (say monthly) should be held at which the service levels and service quality are reviewed by the SCT with the provider's nominated FM Manager. If required business managers (users) can also be present.

The format of these meetings and the topics for discussion should be agreed at an early stage between the SCT and the FM provider. More detailed guidance is provided in 5.1.1.

3.1.4.4 Non-adherence to SLAs

The methods and frequency of monitoring and reporting adherence to SLAs must be stated in the SSR (see 3.1.6.1). Guidance on SLA monitoring is available in the IT Infrastructure Library **Service Level Management** module. To reflect the SLAs in the contract the conditions of CC88 need to be adapted to include service level criteria. Non-compliance must result in the enforcement of financial remedies, for example application of service credits, as defined in the contract.

It is, however, important to be clear about the respective responsibilities of the different parties. If for instance functional errors arise from software developed by a third party, correction might be outside the FM contract and be the responsibility of the SCT. Inadequate response times could be caused by greater demand on the service than that allowed for in the SLA.

Contractual provisions for financial redress can help ensure an effective level of service. However, avoid situations where penalty conditions lead to constant argument over the interpretation of service level figures. This wastes management time and undermines the working relationship between the FM providers and the organization's staff without achieving the service levels required. (Users of CCTA's guidance on Service Level Management and CC88 contracts will find they are framed in such a way that these types of disputes are unlikely.)

3.1.4.5 Process Quality and Auditing

The bases of an FM contract are the SLAs.The contract must also state the procedures used by the FM provider to meet the SLAs. The SCT is responsible for ensuring that the FM provider has a set of systematic procedures for the functions handed over to FM, including for example:

* Problem Management

* Computer Operations Management

* Change Management

* Configuration Management

* Capacity Management

* Contingency Planning

* Availability Management

* Help Desk

* Network Management

* Service Level Management

* User Liaison.

The FM provider should maintain a library of documents relating to its operational quality procedures.

The SCT should audit the FM provider's activities for compliance to stated procedures. These audits should take place frequently - at least once a quarter.

For further guidance on process auditing please refer to the relevant IT Infrastructure Library modules.

The quality of the FM provider's processes, as revealed by audits, should be discussed at the service review meetings described earlier and any required remedial action agreed.

Where a comparatively small team such as the SCT monitors a large organization there is a risk of collusion, albeit unintentional. To guard against this, organizations should consider having an independent review carried out at least annually (eg by other providers, external management consultants or computer auditors).

If the FM provider has obtained third party certification to ISO 9001, it will also be subject to 6-monthly surveillance by the accredited certification body.

**3.1.4.6 Plan Independent
Annual Review**

The independent annual review should cover all aspects of the IT service and of its provision:

* the quality of the service provided to the organization, as defined in the FM contract and SLAs

* adherence to the declared IT infrastructure management procedures

* effectiveness of the SCT (see 5.1.3)

* suggested improvements.

The SCT is responsible for regularly reviewing the organization's use of IT with the FM provider and for initiating changes in its forward IT requirements (see 5.1). It is desirable to have these IT requirements scrutinized by the independent review team.

The results of the independent review are passed to the organization's senior management and the SCT. The SCT is responsible for instigating any follow up action required. It is sensible to use this review as a constituent part of an internal annual review of IT to the Steering Committee. This internal review could also contain:

* review of the overall performance and efficiency of the FM provider

* proposals by SCT for any corrective action

* forward plans.

3.1.4.7 Cost Accounting

It must be possible to audit the activity of the FM providers and the organization's use of IT resource in order to identify and apportion costs incurred in running the customer's workload.

An agreed method is needed to:

* provide an audit trail

* provide suitable accounting statistics.

(See the IT Infrastructure Library module on **Cost Management for IT Services** for more details).

3.1.5 Plan Hand-over Activities

The SSR should be framed to require the FM provider to define a hand-over plan. This enables a smooth changeover of providers, should it ever be necessary. The hand-over plan includes provision for:

* the new provider to have access for 30 to 90 days prior to transfer

* the old provider to train the new provider's staff (especially 'hands on')

* staffing (to ensure enough of the old provider's skilled staff remain during the hand-over).

Most staff planning concerned with individuals, and who is to transfer to the new provider, can be done only after a definite decision has been made to hand over to a new FM provider.

Transfer and conversion of software between machines may pose a problem when changing FM providers. If this is necessary it is important to ensure that either the old FM provider or the organization makes adequate plans to eliminate (or at least ease) any possible problems. Take into account copyright and intellectual property rights issues in relation to bespoke applications. Advice is available from CCTA.

It is vital that during the hand-over adequate backout plans are in place to ensure the continued availability of service if this phase is not successfully completed. See 4.1.3 for more details.

Final payment to the old FM provider must be dependent on the successful completion of the contract ie hand over to a new provider, successfully carried out by the old provider (even if not successfully taken over by the new provider).

The responsibilities of the SCT during hand-over should be to:

* ensure that the organization's business objectives are supported (ie SLAs continue to be met)

* ensure that the old FM provider provides support and training to the new provider

* oversee and, where appropriate, accept on the organization's behalf any software, hardware, accommodation or environmental changes required, and ensure these changes and any amended procedures are completed in time for the new FM provider to begin providing the required services

* carry out quality audits of the state of the IT service, and of the FM providers' procedures and plans, before and after handover.

3.1.6 The Procurement Process

The procurement process for FM is described in the following sub-paragraphs. A diagrammatic representation of the relationship between SLRs, SSRs, SLAs and contracts is given in figure 5.

3.1.6.1 Draw up a Statement of Service Requirement

Once the planning activities outlined in the previous paragraphs of section 3 have been carried out a Statement of Service Requirement (SSR) should be prepared for sending to prospective FM providers. It is important that the SSR is authorized at an appropriate level within the organization. The SSR must contain details of all the services to be run and functions to be managed by the FM provider, and the reports and controls that the organization requires to manage the relationship with the FM provider. The SSR can be a composite of several business requirements.

For FM, CCTA has a contract framework available which can be adapted to form a basis for contracts for the provision of IT services. This adapting is a far from trivial task, which needs to be considered at the SSR stage and progressed throughout the procurement cycle. Too much

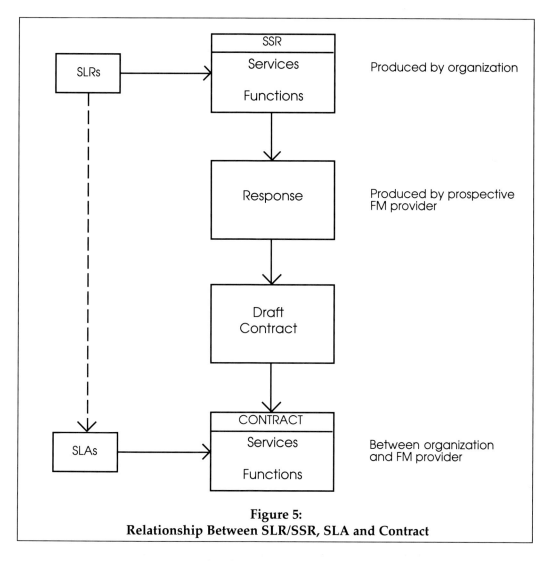

Figure 5:
Relationship Between SLR/SSR, SLA and Contract

detail can lead to a service which is impossible (or uneconomic) to monitor properly, whilst too little can lead to a very loose contract with insufficient protection for the users.

SLRs must be included in the SSR and provide the bulk of the detail for the scheduled workload. If there is a possibility of other user-originated loads, such as internal development or ad hoc batch work that are not covered in SLRs, these must be defined as precisely as possible. It is, however, strongly recommended that all such workloads **are** covered by SLRs.

If, as is likely to be recommended by CCTA, Appendix B or C of CC88 part 2-C is used as appropriate, with provisions for service charge abatement and liquidated damages (and, in the case of C, Breach of Contract) the need for the users to adhere to their part of the SLA becomes paramount. Failure to adhere could nullify any claims against the FM provider.

It is important to ensure that the SSR contains the requirements rather than the solutions (eg 'process 1000 unemployment benefit query transactions per hour' not 'use distributed DRS 30s to collect data and transmit via PSS to....'). Any known or expected deadlines, eg payable orders to be produced by 1600 hours each day, must be included in the SSR. There is no reason why existing or preferred solutions should not be included but this must not be at the expense of the basic requirements, nor confused with them.

As in all negotiations of this type, it is important to remember that the contractual levels are the **minimum** acceptable, not necessarily what you may expect as normal. On the other hand these minimum levels could be provided for weeks on end without contractual redress - so do not specify service levels that you cannot live with.

Overall cost-effectiveness (including user productivity benefits) should decide the levels at which to set service requirements. For existing services, the acceptability and cost of past service levels are a good indicator of what is reasonable.

Consider specifying IT availability and performance targets for both short and long term periods. The short term target affords the organization the ability to raise with a service provider cases of poor service provision, close to the time they occur, with a view to achieving a timely improvement. The longer term target allows the service provider the facility to absorb 'a bad month' and still achieve acceptable availability and performance over a longer period.

For example, it would not be unreasonable to commit a service provider to contract to 99% availability over a 6 month period, but for availability during any one of the constituent months only 96% or better. If requirements are over specified (especially the short term targets) this can lead to very costly solutions or the need to reissue an SSR if no provider can meet all the mandatory requirements. The SCT should consider the use of availability and capacity planning techniques to arrive at reasonable figures (see the IT Infrastructure Library **Availability Management** and **Capacity Management** modules).

A statement of the security requirements to be observed by the FM provider must be included in the SSR and should cover the eight aspects of security:

*   hardware

*   software

*   physical

*   procedural

*   personnel

*   environmental

*   communications

*   tempest (shielding electronic emissions).

Organizations must also state any specific conditions about how their security requirements should be met eg possible requirement for a dedicated machine. However, security is costly and the organization should ensure that any security requirements are realistic and are driven by a business requirement. It is recommended that organizations use, and require FM providers to use, CCTA's Risk Analysis and Management Method (CRAMM) to assess their threats and vulnerabilities and provide options for countering them. For more details on CRAMM please contact CCTA.

Security is sometimes cited as a reason for locating the equipment at an organization's own site. This argument, however, is valid only for the most sensitive workloads. (The US Government believes the security to be sufficiently adequate to use FM, both on and off site, for much of the IT support for its Space Programme).

The SSR should state that the FM provider must use systematic processes for all IT Infrastructure Management functions. It is desirable that FM providers should use IT Infrastructure Library practices and principles in preference to proprietary methods. Alternatively, prospective providers should supply details of their procedures for IT Infrastructure Library (ITIL) functions, to demonstrate that these procedures are functionally equivalent to ITIL procedures.

The organization and/or its representative should regularly audit the FM provider's activities as described in 3.1.4. The FM provider is contractually required fully to cooperate with the organization or its representative in connection with these audits.

The duration of the contract must be stated. To keep the organization's options open, CCTA recommends that in general it is best to limit the maximum term of the contract to five years. However, there are cases where for sound policy reasons the contract period should be longer - an example of this is where the recovery of costs by the FM provider over a five year period, for a large initial capital investment in equipment, would make the cost excessive.

Decide whether the contract should be subject to annual renewal by the organization after the second year. The cost to an FM provider of taking over service provision would make it unlikely that a contract for less than 2 years would be viable. However, where FM is being used to run an existing service while a new one is being introduced, or to provide a small part of the service, the minimum contractual period may be shorter.

For further information on the content of SSRs please contact CCTA.

3.1.6.2 Seek Competitive Proposals and Shortlist Bidders

There is a standard competitive tender process used by government organizations to select providers. An SSR (see 3.1.6.1) is produced by the organization and made available to prospective providers. Responses to the SSR by prospective providers are evaluated and a shortlist of providers, perhaps 2 or 3, is drawn up.

Shortlisting of Bidders

The selection of an FM provider should follow the procurement procedures set out in the CCTA IS Guides on FM and Procurement. The scope of an FM contract introduces a greater degree of complexity than is present for most other examples of IT system or service procurement.

In addition to taking account of costs, organizations should consider the following whilst shortlisting prospective providers:

* size and stability of the provider

* previous track-record as an FM provider

* flexibility of approach (eg to changes, problems, contingencies etc)

* experience in other relevant IT areas

* whether the provider's resources are shared or dedicated

* personnel policies and specifically their policy on take-on of existing staff (the organization should discuss this with the Trade Unions as early as practicable).

CCTA can supply information on many prospective providers.

It is good practice to require all short-listed FM providers to give a presentation on their company and its proposals. The FM provider's nominated FM Manager should attend this presentation.

The organization needs to know whether its existing staff are to be offered employment with the FM provider. Experience indicates that on transfer of the work from one provider to another it is normal for 80% or more of staff to transfer to the new provider.

The following information should be sought from proposed providers about their key personnel:

* their commitment/availability

* their educational and professional qualifications

* their present role

* relationships between the proposed job and others they have done

* why they are competent to do this job (eg their claimed experience and understanding of current requirements).

Conduct interviews similar to job interviews with the shortlisted providers' key personnel (those with key skills who are to be supplied by the provider) to verify and supplement this information.

Assurance on the following points is needed from the shortlisted providers:

* that there is provider commitment as to which members of staff will be supplied (ie key personnel)

* that key personnel understand they have been proposed to work on the project and intend to take up the post if the provider's tender is successful

* that these key personnel are available.

Organizations must also consider whether the FM provider's staff need security vetting and if there is a requirement for them to sign the Official Secrets Act.

Note that the FM provider's staff are likely to change during the course of the FM contract. The quality of the company and its personnel policies are therefore just as important as assurances on specific personnel.

It is important that prospective providers supply evidence of the processes they propose to use to meet the requirements. Organizations should obtain as much proof as possible to substantiate prospective providers' claims that they can 'do the job'.

For example:

* examine documentation

* visit sites

* interview existing customers

* carry out interviews to prove the prospective providers understand all IT infrastructure management principles.

If an FM provider is not willing to commit to using IT Infrastructure Library practices and principles, or procedures based on broadly similar principles, organizations should consider the viability of proceeding further in the contractual process with that provider.

3.1.6.3 The Contract

In Government procurement the Memorandum of Agreement (MOA) is normally a prerequisite to signing a contract. However, experience has shown that in contracting for FM it is more appropriate to move directly from evaluation of providers' responses to the SSR to a draft contract stage. This section gives guidance on a number of subjects that must be considered at the draft contract stage, which may result in inclusions in the final contract.

If personnel and other resources are to be transferred to the FM provider, the numbers and terms on which they are to be taken on need to be agreed.

Where the hardware covered by the FM agreement is owned or leased by the organization, it is often sold, or the lease transferred, to the FM provider. Unless the organization specifies a requirement for a dedicated machine (eg on security grounds) the FM provider might use the hardware for other contracts. Sharing of resources could be of financial advantage to the organization.

There are a number of options regarding the ownership of computer hardware. The following types of equipment might be owned by either the FM provider or the organization:

* the central computer systems

* remote workstations linked to the computer systems

* free standing mini or microcomputers or those linked to a Local Area Network (LAN)

* Wide Area Networks

* LANs and their servers

* cabling.

Accommodation and the environmental infrastructure may also be owned by either the provider or the organization.

For any FM contract there could be a mix of ownership between the FM provider and the organization. A common example is for the FM provider to own the central computer systems and premises on which they are sited and the organization to retain ownership of the free standing microcomputers in users' offices.

Where the FM provider is required to supply a total IT service bound by SLAs, it may be better if all the hardware and accommodation is owned by the FM provider, as this places all the onus on the provider. Whatever the exact circumstances, it is important to specify clearly which items are being transferred to the FM provider and which still belongs to the organization. This obviates any future disputes over ownership (see 3.1.7 for guidance on software matters).

Whoever owns the IT and environmental infrastructure, future responsibility for administration of contracts and agreements for the supply and maintenance of hardware, software and environmental facilities must be clearly stipulated in the contract. Where the FM provider is to be responsible, which is usual, the organization will wish to satisfy itself that maintenance contracts, support agreements etc that the FM provider enters into are adequate.

33

Acceptance criteria for the testing of an FM service need to be agreed at draft contract stage: see 4.1.1.

The FM provider may propose converting a system to run on different hardware. Any such change must go through the normal change management system; see 5.1.4 for more information. The organization needs to be satisfied on the cost (if any) of the conversion, and that adequate safeguards are provided to ensure continuity of the service beyond the end of the FM contract, ie that the organization does not become locked into a proprietary system. If a conversion does go ahead the organization may itself have to (or it may have to place a contract to) convert application software systems. In this case, the organization is responsible for overseeing the satisfactory, and timely, conversion.

It must be made clear in the negotiations on the draft contract, and the final contract must reflect, that the provision of an FM service consists of at least 3 phases:

*   start-up, during which the new FM provider will be working alongside and receive training from the organization's and/or the old FM provider's staff

*   the service provision phase during which the FM provider is responsible for providing the IT service

*   hand-over, during which the old FM provider will be working alongside and training the organization's and/or the new FM provider's staff - see figure 4 (page 19).

The requirements in the SLAs should be reflected in the service level provisions of the FM contract (eg CC88 part 2C, and appropriate Appendix). The SLAs should also be appended to the contract as a schedule.

The methods of monitoring, reporting and reviewing SLAs must be stipulated in the contract. SLA reports should be produced at least weekly, and formal reviews held monthly. The contract should make clear the organization's rights to audit the FM provider's activities - using, when required, an independent organization.

It should be stated in the contract how changes (eg to SLRs/SLAs) will be charged for (see also 5.1.4). This may be by stipulating any or all of the following:

*   daily rates (eg price per programmer, analyst or operator day)

* service charges (including hardware enhancements, maintenance, software etc).

* fixed price quotation.

For many changes there is a running cost difference as well as a cost associated with development and implementation. The contract should make clear the basis of charging for each of these two phases. Note that the contract may include the availability of some staff and other resources before any charges are levied.

The contract must contain information on charge reductions where there are decreases in the service provided, as well as charge increases where there are increases in the service.

CC88 part 5A gives details of principles and procedures for change control in contracts.

Forms of contractual redress for poor service may include:

* service charge credits

* liquidated damages (as a percentage of the total service charges) which can be scaled according to importance of transaction/service.

Other possible contractual safeguards include:

* ability to test/validate any changes against an agreed benchmark

* acceptance based on CC88 part 3A (procedures for acceptance testing)

* a formal method of price revision

* designated 6-or 12-monthly points when SLAs can be reviewed, and contract charges adjusted.

Advice on the duration of contracts is given in 3.4.2.

It is beyond the scope of this module to provide great detail on contractual matters. However, further details on all procurement matters including the types of contract (eg fixed cost, cost plus time and materials) available can be obtained from CCTA and also from the CCTA IS Guides on Procurement and FM. Annex D contains a synopsis of items to be considered for inclusion in a draft FM contract.

3.1.7 Implications for Software Operation, Development and Maintenance

In general it is good practice to discuss the acceptability of application software with any potential FM provider at an early stage. If there are any doubts about the quality of the software the FM provider may be unwilling to run it without improvements, which would probably have to be funded by the organization. The organization may find that the FM provider is unwilling to maintain poor quality software, which could mean that another contractor would have to be funded to do so.

During the life of the FM contract new applications software and systems are likely to be required and appropriate provision needs to be made in the contract. It is normally the responsibility of the organization to decide on the sourcing of new applications and applications software enhancements.

Applications development/maintenance might be carried out by:

* the organization

* the FM provider

* a commercial software/systems supplier.

In all three of the above possibilities, performance, reliability, availability, security and other service level requirements form part of the system specification and these should be in a form which can be incorporated within an SLA.

When new software is installed, the SLAs associated with the FM service may need to be extended or amended. Further information on this subject is available in the **Service Level Management** module.

If applications development is to be provided by the FM provider, the FM provider should use SSADM for systems analysis and design. This ensures that applications are designed to agreed standards of manageability and operability. It also simplifies the process of choosing a provider as differing design management methods will not have to be assessed and compared.

The organization should require the FM provider to use PRINCE, the CCTA-recommended project management method.

Application maintenance/support might be carried out by:

* the FM provider

* a computer software/system supplier

* the organization.

It is likely that, in general, organizations will find it attractive to use the FM provider who is, after all, responsible for running the software and adhering to SLAs, to maintain application software.

The responsibilities of the software supplier need to be distinguished from those of the software maintainer, since separate contracts are likely to be involved. The software supplier's responsibility is to deliver a quality product on time. The software maintainer has the responsibility to test that the software is acceptable to maintain and then to maintain it in accordance with any support agreement. It should be made clear in the contract that the FM provider has a responsibility to install application software (if so required by the organization) and run it.

If the organization requires the FM provider to maintain software it did not develop, the organization will wish to satisfy itself that the FM provider is competent to do so.

If another party is to maintain software the FM provider will wish to have a support contract with the application maintainer that is sufficiently tight to support the FM provider's adherence to SLAs. The organization should satisfy itself that this support contract is satisfactory.

New applications software will normally be licensed to the FM provider for operation of the system. Charges for the software licence will be passed on to the organization in the form of additional FM service charges.

3.2 Dependencies

All the planning activities outlined in 3.1 should be carried out. Especially important are the plans for:

* SLAs

* ongoing management

* start-up and handover

and the items detailed below in 3.2.

3.2.1 Hardware and Environment

It is essential at the planning stage to ensure that the proposed hardware and environmental facilities are adequate to support the SLAs. The contract should stipulate who is responsible for the initial provision and the ongoing maintenance/support of hardware and environmental facilities.

3.2.2 Software

Any licences for proprietary software will normally become the responsibility of the FM provider. However, the ability of current IT service providers to reassign software licences to an FM provider may be at the discretion of the software copyright owner. Early negotiation with the software copyright owners is necessary if the FM provider may be required to run licensed software.

Ensure that the FM provider has adequate maintenance agreements for any software taken over/provided.

3.2.3 Staff

The successful transfer of work and continuing quality of IT service, supplied by an FM provider, depend on the availability of suitably qualified and committed staff from the FM provider.

The successful planning of FM requires that the FM project and the SCT are staffed as early as possible with suitably qualified people.

3.3 People

Staffing issues have potential impact throughout the organization's IT Directorate - particularly the IT Services Section. (See figure 2, page 9, for details of areas likely to be affected). It is essential that internal staffing issues are handled sensitively and reasonably.

For guidance on issues associated with the FM provider's staff please see section 3.1.6.2.

3.3.1 Current IT Staff

Where the FM provider takes over an existing service, the organization's staff are often offered employment with the FM provider, frequently on similar terms of contract. Where staff are to be transferred to the FM provider, it is important to encourage staff support for the move.

The following measures might be considered:

* persuade the FM provider to offer all existing staff continued employment

* tackle any concerns regarding continued rights (eg pensions or sick pay) internally, using the organization's Personnel Section

* inform staff when the best package has been negotiated with the provider

* highlight the benefits of transferring to the FM provider (see section 6).

In general any problems that can be dealt with centrally (ie at organization rather than personal level) should be sorted out in advance to minimize staff concerns.

Where possible, organizations should consider using their internal IT staff on any new work. This is likely to provide the following benefits:

* new skills for the organization's staff (benefit to both organization and staff)

* feeling of working at or nearer to the 'leading edge'

* higher morale and job satisfaction (and consequential effects, eg reduced absenteeism and lower staff turnover).

A short term disadvantage could be the time and cost required to train the organization's staff.

The organization should include the Trade Unions as early as practicable in discussions about current IT staff and how they will be affected.

In essence, enlightened management is more likely to alleviate adverse reaction by ensuring that it acts in the best interests of the staff.

3.3.2 Service Control Team (SCT)

To manage the organization's side of the relationship with the FM provider, the organization should retain a level of expertise in a Service Control Team, headed by one of the organization's senior IT Managers. The role and size of the SCT are discussed in detail in 3.1.2.

3.3.3 Training

To achieve the required quality of IT service the SCT and FM provider's staff need to be trained in the principles and practices of the IT Infrastructure Library.

In addition SCT staff need training in auditing, inter-personal relationship skills and negotiating skills.

3.4 Timing

For existing operations the elapsed time from deciding to move to FM through to start up of the FM service, is likely to be between 6 and 18 months. For greenfield operations, a longer planning period is required.

3.4.1 Start-up & hand-over

Figure 4, page 19, shows the sequence of start-up and hand-over when the responsibility for the IT service is being passed from internal staff to an FM provider, and then on to another FM provider.

3.4.2 Duration of Contract

Although FM contractors are interested in as long a contract as possible, they would probably contract for as short a period as required. However, the original disruption, familiarization and capital outlay mean that it is likely to be impractical or expensive for them to contract for short periods. One possible exception to this is where FM is used as a means of allowing migration to a new system.

The duration of FM contracts generally varies from 1 year to indefinite with reviews and termination clauses. CCTA advises that to keep the organization's options open the contractual commitment from the FM provider should be 5 years, and that from the organization 2 years, each being able to terminate thereafter on 12 months notice. However, the pricing implications on large contracts may lead to longer term contracts and reciprocity of commitment. Annual internal reviews will decide whether the FM services and the performance of the FM provider are of a satisfactory quality.

A further consideration is to ensure that the termination of an FM contract does not coincide with other major changes in the organization.

Consideration must be given as to the duration and termination conditions of existing contracts (eg maintenance agreements, equipment leases).

More details on procurement matters are given in 3.1.6.

4. Implementation

This section deals with implementing the plans described in section 3.

4.1 Procedures

4.1.1 Start-up/hand-over

During the start-up/hand-over the plans outlined in section 3 must be implemented. All staff involved in or affected by the move to FM should by now be clear about any changes that will take place and how these changes may affect them.

During this period either the organization's staff or the old FM provider's staff work alongside the new FM provider's key personnel. The new staff should be in place between 30 and 90 days before the FM provider commences IT service provision. During this period the old provider's staff carry out on the job training for any new staff.

The new FM provider's staff, assisted and overseen by the SCT, work to achieve the smooth transfer of service provision. This is done by ensuring that:

* all necessary software and documentation are transferred to the FM provider

* administration of all relevant hardware and maintenance contracts or leases is transferred to, or contract renegotiations completed by, the FM provider

* staff to be employed by the FM provider are completely clear about their conditions of employment and are informed of their new roles and responsibilities

* all contractual requirements concerning the move to the new FM provider are met and the FM provider assumes responsibility for the relevant systems and services.

The FM provider's functions and services must be scrutinized, tested and accepted by the organization. If the contract is based on CC88 rules, the conditions in part 3-A of that document may be adapted for the acceptance testing of an FM service. The procedures stipulate the running of a user workload for a specified period, 20 days being usual for any sizeable system. As written, 3-A criteria are based only on achieving specified service levels for a defined minimum configuration. In the case of FM ensure that the overall quality of the various services is acceptable. Criteria need to be agreed, prior to contract, based on service level and any other requirements that are to be made contractually binding. Setting these criteria when transferring a stable workload from one FM provider to another is relatively straightforward but some care needs to be exercised for systems that are being extensively developed or are growing quickly. The initial workload may not be representative of that on which the contract is based, and some simulated loading may be necessary.

Where practical, consider the use of parallel running, ie keeping the old provider on standby for a period after the new provider 'goes live'. Even if the change of provider involves changing to a new system, thus making parallel running less practical, care should be taken to ensure that short term backout is still possible (see 4.1.3). It is very important during this high risk period that adequate contingency plans are in place.

The changeover to the new provider occurs smoothly only if everyone concerned is kept fully informed. All changes to procedures must be subject to change management (involving the SCT) and if necessary notified to the users in good time. Consider whether the Help Desk needs any additional support during this phase to deal with user queries.

4.1.2 Controlling the Service

During start-up, the procedures for monitoring the service and auditing the processes must be implemented and tested. (These procedures should also be used for acceptance testing the service). The new FM provider puts tools and mechanisms into place for monitoring the service, and demonstrates them to the SCT to prove that they work. The new FM provider then installs its IT infrastructure management processes, on which the SCT carries out a trial audit.

It is recommended that the SCT also carries out (or arranges to be carried out) an audit of the state of the IT infrastructure before and after handover.

Although it is the responsibility of the FM provider to measure and supply information on the service levels achieved, organizations must be confident that the statistics being produced adequately represent the service being provided. Provision should be made for the organization to monitor the service by having access to the FM provider's tools.

Service review meetings should be instigated during implementation and held at least monthly thereafter. At these meetings the SCT reviews the quality of provided IT service and discusses future plans for the service with the FM provider. It is essential to have the commitment of the organization's management to monitoring and reviewing the service. See 3.1.4.3 for details of the scope and purpose of these meetings and the necessary management information to be supplied by the FM provider.

During the review meetings the quality of the processes used to provide the IT service, as revealed from process audits, should also be discussed, and any required remedial action agreed.

4.1.3 Backout

In case handover to a new FM provider fails, the organization must have a fall-back position to ensure it can continue to run its IT services.

In the case of a backout the SCT could act as a nucleus of expertise in IT and experience in the work of the organization. However this approach is fraught with problems. The national IT skills shortage will almost certainly prevent the organization immediately staffing the IT Directorate with enough permanent staff of the right calibre. Besides, the organization may have neither sufficient IT accommodation nor hardware / software of the right type. If, however, the FM service was being provided from the organization's own location, and ownership of the software / hardware can be transferred to the organization, expertise can possibly be bought in to staff the IT Directorate. This expertise is likely to be in the form of consultants and contract programmers / operators, at least until in-house staff can be recruited and trained.

If some of the organization's own staff were transferred to the FM provider, the contract should allow for the organization to re-employ them. In general, however, it would be better to employ the second choice FM provider.

4.2 Dependencies

4.2.1 Hardware and Environment

The organization must satisfy itself that:

* the hardware and environmental facilities are transferred to the FM provider

* responsibility for any contracts applying to the supply or maintenance of hardware and environmental facilities is taken on by the FM provider

and that these are done on time and in accordance with any stipulations in the FM contract.

The hardware and environment, and contracts for their supply and maintenance, must be adequate to support the SLAs.

4.2.2 Software

The organization needs to be satisfied that all relevant software licences are being transferred to the FM provider, or that the FM provider has renegotiated the licences, and that this is done with effect from the date on which the FM provider assumes responsibility for the IT services.

If the FM provider's staff are not already familiar with the operation and support of all appropriate software, appropriate training needs to be provided. Responsibility for providing and funding any such training will have been identified in the FM contract.

The FM provider will normally wish to carry out a check or acceptance test of all software handed over by the organization. This is in the interest of the organization, to help ensure quality IT Services.

If another third party is responsible for application support and maintenance, the FM provider must have agreed, contractually, support and maintenance targets with the maintainers, for fixing faults and answering enquiries.

4.2.3 Key Personnel

The successful transfer of responsibility for the IT service is dependent on the old and new FM providers' key personnel being available from the beginning of the start-up and hand-over phases.

4.2.4 Testing and handover

The organization is dependent on adequate testing and handover plans and procedures to ensure a quality service is supplied/maintained. More information on testing and handover is given in 3.1 and 4.1.

4.2.5 Monitoring and Auditing

Tools and procedures for monitoring the quality of provided IT service, and to support audits of the FM provider's procedures, are required.

4.3 People

It is important to ensure that all users and staff are aware of the move to FM and are kept up to date during the implementation phase. A convenient way of doing this is through a regular newsletter which would initially introduce the plans and timetables for the implementation, and later give notification of specific changes to procedures or relocation of facilities, such as the Help Desk.

If the move to FM is expected to cause changes in staffing or procedures, management should consider arranging meetings to explain the reasons for the changes, with question and answer sessions.

4.4 Timing

The Start-up and Hand-over phases should be implemented as described in 3.1.3, 3.1.5 and figure 4.

Start-up should begin 30 - 90 days before commencement of service.

Shortly before and after hand-over the SCT should formally audit the IT infrastructure and the new provider's documentation and procedures. The SCT might exceptionally recommend backout before or during formal acceptance testing. As previously stated, it is recommended that the old provider's staff should still be available for a short period (eg 5-10 days) after the new provider 'goes live'.

5. Post-implementation and Audit

This section deals with the ongoing monitoring and reviews needed when managing an FM provider.

5.1 Procedures

5.1.1 Monitoring the SLAs

SLAs are a basis for the contract of service agreed between the FM provider and the customer organization. Adherence to SLAs is the main indication that the FM provider is operating a successful service and that the users are keeping their demands within agreed limits.

Service review meetings (covered in more detail later in this section) should be held monthly. At these reviews, the SCT formally liaises with the FM provider's personnel. User representatives should attend some or all of the meetings. The service provided is measured against the SLAs and trends identified and analyzed. Attention is paid to trending not just fluctuations in the quality of service provided but also changes in the pattern of use. The reviews take a forward look at future workload, service, and usage requirements.

Satisfactory service levels for the periods under review are those within previously agreed bounds, that do not cause the budget to be exceeded or the SLAs to be violated. Corrective action is needed where service levels are unsatisfactory.

There are likely to be two major reasons for service levels not being met. Either the FM provider is not performing to specification, or the users have increased their workload requirement. In the first case it is most important to establish what the FM provider intends to do to improve the service. A remedial action plan must be agreed and implemented and the SCT should instigate the necessary contractual controls. In the second case it may be necessary to renegotiate the SLAs. This will almost certainly involve an increase in cost (see 5.1.4).

The FM contract should define when and how financial remedies are applied following the contractor's failure to meet agreed service level criteria. Although these remedies do not always fully compensate for the loss of service they should concentrate the mind of the FM provider on improving services in the future (see 3.1.4.4 for more details).

5.1.1.1 Management Reports

The organization requires regular and frequent management reports from the FM provider. These reports should be produced weekly, monthly and quarterly with comparisons against the previous period(s). There must also be a mechanism for producing exception reports and urgent reports (see below).

All items within SLAs and any items required by the organization (whether subject to contractual criteria or not) must be reflected in the reports eg:

* availability

* reliability

* average and maximum peak hour response times

* number of functional errors in each service, and impact level

* average and maximum number of users during the peak hour

* peak hour transaction rate

* batch job throughput

* attempted security violations and follow up action taken

* Help Desk call statistics

* number of changes requested and implemented

* number of incidents/problems initiated/closed.

It is the responsibility of the FM provider to supply information to the SCT regarding the service levels achieved. However, organizations must be confident that the statistics being produced accurately represent the service being provided. It is therefore recommended that the SCT has regular demonstrations of the use of FM provider's IT infrastructure management software tools (and, by arrangement, also hands-on access to them) on the actual system used to provide the IT service. One method of validating some of the statistics produced is to arrange, perhaps via the Help Desk, for a representative sample of users manually to monitor availability, response times and other aspects of service quality. These records can then be compared with the FM provider's records at regular intervals.

Management Reports should be dealt with in the following way:

* normal reports - sent to SCT and reviewed at service review meetings. Any significant trends or problems may result in an urgent meeting being convened and/or result in a change request being raised

* exception reports (typically due to non-compliance with SLAs) sent to the SCT with an explanation of what went wrong together with the corrective action being proposed or implemented. An urgent meeting may be required to discuss the proposed or implemented changes

* urgent reports - the FM provider should convene a meeting with the SCT to explain the situation and discuss any proposed or implemented remedy.

5.1.1.2 Service review meetings

The service levels and quality should be reviewed by the SCT at regular meetings (eg monthly) with the provider's nominated FM Manager. If required business managers can also be present. The major topics for discussion at these meetings will be:

* review of service achievements

* review of service quality measures (eg quantity and seriousness of incidents/problems)

* review of service related problems

* identification of service trends

* workload projections

* summary of changes carried out

* identification of the need for minor changes to the service (if approved these would be processed using normal change management procedures)

* initiation of any major changes (eg capacity upgrade, procedural change) including financial implications (see 5.1.4).

The SCT must ensure that any follow up actions or remedial plans are implemented.

It is recommended that at least twice a year service review meetings are convened with user/business managers present. As well as reviewing the provided services the meetings should look ahead and decide requirements for the future of the services. The planning horizon should be set sufficiently far ahead (eg 12 to 24 months) to take account of lead times for capacity upgrades and IT infrastructure changes, including the time needed to obtain management approval for additional funds. A fully documented record of service review meetings should be maintained.

The SCT should satisfy itself, off-line if necessary, that the business and technical assumptions behind the FM provider's tactical planning (eg capacity plans) are soundly-based, and take remedial action if not.

The organization's requirements with regard to security should be reviewed:

* regularly, eg every 6 months

* immediately upon being notified of a significant change in the security requirements

* after any security breach.

This review ensures that the level of security afforded by the FM provider can be changed, if need be, to reflect the organization's new requirements. This may involve the organization in increased expenditure. The use of CCTA's Risk Analysis and Management Method CRAMM facilitates such a review.

5.1.2 Auditing the Processes

At least once a year, a service review summary should be presented to the organization's IS Steering Committee for information and for ratification of any required changes (see 5.1.4).

The SCT is responsible for auditing the processes used to achieve the required service levels. The FM provider must adhere to agreed procedures and must conform to any agreed security requirements. As indicated in 3.1 and 4.1, details of the FM provider's procedures are available to the SCT. Frequent audits (at least quarterly) should be undertaken and fully documented by the organization. For guidance on auditing each of the IT Infrastructure Library disciplines please refer to the relevant module.

For guidance on a general approach to auditing all IT infrastructure management activities please refer to the **Quality Audit** module.

Consideration should be given to the use of an independent third party to audit for compliance with the procedures and to review the FM provider's performance on a less frequent basis (at least annually).

Audits should also be carried out:

* in the case of protracted poor service

* if the procedures are significantly changed.

A report must be produced following every audit of the FM provider.

The results of any audits should be discussed at the regular service quality meetings, with any remedial action being agreed and initiated, including the amendment of procedures as appropriate.

5.1.3 Review Effectiveness and Efficiency of SCT

The SCT must review its own efficiency and effectiveness by setting metrics, and regularly measuring and documenting how well it carries out its responsibilities. Section 3.1.2 has details of the responsibility of the SCT. Examples of metrics are:

* number and seriousness of user problems due to training programme/strategy

* number and seriousness of technical planning problems

* number and seriousness of problems caused by faulty processes on the part of the FM provider, not picked up by the SCT

* number and seriousness of problems caused by poor support or maintenance contracts, not picked up via SCT audits

* number of problems attributed to business analysis/planning.

In addition the independent review carried out annually (see 3.1.4 and 5.1.6 for more information) should review the efficiency and effectiveness of the SCT.

5.1.4 Change Management

IT Infrastructure Library change management procedures should be used. The SCT must be represented on the change advisory board. For more details of managing change refer to the IT Infrastructure Library module **Change Management**.

The service contract allows for changes to the amount and utilization of the IT infrastructure and staff resources. The method of charging to implement and operate such changes must be stipulated in the contract. The FM provider's charges should be monitored and compared with current market rates. The more contentious part of the costing of changes may be predicting the number of days effort required to carry out a change. The SCT needs to have sufficient expertise to negotiate on these matters with the FM provider.

It must be recognized that all changes (including any fed in from the capacity planning process) will be charged for if the FM provider needs to supply extra IT or staff resources, over and above those provided for under the contract, to implement or operate the change (see 3.1.6.3 for details). It should be remembered, however, that a reduction in resources required will not necessarily produce corresponding cost savings for the organization, unless provided for in the contract.

It is the SCT's responsibility to ensure that changes to procedures do not lead to the organization becoming locked in to a single FM provider. This responsibility can best be achieved by ensuring that non-proprietary quality procedures (eg as documented in the IT Infrastructure Library) are followed.

The regular forward looks at service, application and usage plans will result in user/SCT requests for change. The SCT may be given delegated authority to progress with changes that fall below given 'implementation' and 'operation' cost limits.

Requirements for major changes are fed into the system by the IS Steering Committee or the IT Executive Committee, and requests for changes that would result in expenditure above the limits just mentioned have to be fed back to one of these senior committees for approval. In general this dialogue with senior committees takes place as part of the organization's annual review of IS strategy.

Plans for IT expenditure in the next financial year are generally reviewed in a tactical planning exercise carried out in preparation for the organization's annual financial planning (in Government terms, for submission of supply estimates). Changes expected in the next financial year - whether imposed by the strategy committees or identified via service reviews - are fed into this tactical planning exercise and those that are approved are fed to the FM provider to implement, subject to normal change management and scheduling conditions.

5.1.5 IT Infrastructure Enhancements

Decisions concerning the organization's strategy and funding of new IT systems and services, and enhancements to existing systems and services, must be taken by the organization itself, although advice is likely to be sought from the FM provider. For example the final decision on whether to develop new bespoke applications or buy packaged solutions should be taken in-house. For all such systems, plans need to be made for installation and acceptance testing. If the systems are to be developed in-house, plans must be drawn up to manage the development work. If systems are to be bought-in, the organization must plan the procurement or arrange for it to be planned by the FM provider, overseen by the organization.

When the hardware has to be upgraded and/or replaced to meet the organization's requirements (see the IT Infrastructure Library **Capacity Management** module), the organization must ratify the expenditure involved. Even if the hardware is changed to meet the FM provider's requirements, the organization must exercise sufficient control over the new type of hardware to be installed, to safeguard the organization's interests. The SCT must agree acceptance tests for the new hardware and oversee the transfer of work to the new equipment.

The normal change management process ensures all such changes are assessed for their impact on SLAs. All contracts appertaining to new hardware and software must be sufficiently robust to support SLAs: the SCT must satisfy itself of this.

For further information on installation and acceptance testing of bought-in software and new equipment see the IT Infrastructure Library modules on **Software Control and Distribution**, **Computer Installation and Acceptance**, and **Network Management**.

**5.1.5.1 Development and
Procurement of Applications
Software**

From time to time, applications software will have to be developed or procured. The development of new bespoke application software and systems might be carried out by the organization, the FM provider or a third party system supplier.

Even if applications development is undertaken by the FM provider or a third party systems house, suitable project management and systems design methods are required. It is recommended that PRINCE and SSADM are used by FM providers, and other third parties. Use of PRINCE facilitates Government organizations' participation on project boards. Use of SSADM ensures consistency of quality and design with the rest of Government and prevents organizations becoming locked into a single provider using other proprietary methods.

The organization, whilst passing the management and development of applications to an FM provider or third party systems supplier, must not lose control of those applications. The SCT must have membership of the PRINCE project organization, particularly of the project assurance teams.

For applications development projects, change management is of paramount importance. It is imperative that changes to be made within an applications development environment are assessed for impact on the IT infrastructure and vice versa. See the IT Infrastructure Library module on **Change Management** for more details.

Any limitations to be placed on development work during peak periods, to prevent it hampering the running of production work, should be clearly stated to the developer. These limitations should be included in SLAs.

For bespoke and package software, the organization needs to ensure there are formal arrangements to control:

* the quality of the software

* the availability of specialist applications support once the software has been developed

* maintenance of the software

* introduction of new applications to the system.

The formal arrangements should include:

* acceptance criteria concerning functionality, number and severity of known errors, performance, maintainability etc

* rigorous independent test procedures to be applied, independent of applications developers/suppliers, before any new or amended application goes live

* the extent and quality of applications specialist support to be provided (ie on-call technical staff) once the software is in live use

* agreed targets for rectifying faults according to their impact, once the software is in live use.

5.1.5.2 Installation and Acceptance Testing of Applications Software

When a new application system is delivered, the FM provider will probably be responsible for its installation. The organization must ensure that rigorous acceptance testing is carried out. This might be done by the FM provider, in co-operation with the users and the SCT. If the FM provider is not involved in the organization's acceptance testing, it may well wish to carry out its own testing before accepting operational and support responsibility for the new system.

Further detail on controlling application management passed to an FM provider or third party systems supplier can be obtained from CCTA.

5.1.6 Independent Annual Review

Arrange for an independent annual review of all aspects of FM service provision (see 3.1.4.6 for details). Present the results to senior management for their information and the instigation of any corrective action.

5.1.7 Retendering and Renewal

It is necessary to review the overall effectiveness of using FM and report to senior management to enable decisions about renewal of contracts to be made. The regular management reports, service review meetings, and independent annual reviews give some information about the effectiveness of the FM provider.

However, the only real method of comparing costs is to retender the contract competitively. CCTA advises that, in general, the contractual commitment for the FM provider should be 5 years, and that for the organization 2 years, each being able to terminate thereafter on 12 months notice. This gives organizations leverage to ensure that changes are costed competitively. Also planned changes can be included in the renewed contract which obviates the need for additional costs to be incurred later.

It is recommended that, after 5 years, the contract should be re-tendered.

At the end of the FM contract, if the current FM provider is unsuccessful in retendering, the provider will either be:

* handing the service over to a new FM provider or

* returning the service to the organization's IT Directorate (although this option is unlikely).

Ensure that adequate time is allowed for the hand-over period and that new staff are fully trained by the outgoing service provider. The new FM provider's personnel must be on site to manage the hand-over and provide any required information. The old FM provider should also be available for advice during this period. See section 4 for more information.

5.2 Dependencies

5.2.1 Service Level Agreements

The SLAs underpin the contract with the FM provider. Ensure that the SLAs are adhered to by the FM provider, and that they result in the provision of the required service to the user. Where user behaviour and user demands result in SLAs not being adhered to, the requirements of the business should be analyzed and any required changes instigated to ensure these business requirements can be met. The contract must stipulate that regular reviews of service levels and of SLAs take place (see also 5.2.3). To check that SLAs are being adhered to, the necessary monitoring facilities must be in place.

5.2.2 Audit checklists

To have confidence that a quality IT service will be maintained the organization should understand, in general terms, the FM provider's IT infrastructure management processes. The organization should, from time to time, arrange for an audit of the processes, concentrating particularly on areas of known weakness and instigating corrective action where necessary. For example, if an audit shows that projected workload figures are not being correctly translated into capacity plans, this could seriously jeopardize the quality of the IT service some 2 years downstream. Non-adherence to change management or problem management controls could jeopardize IT service quality in the immediate future. These and other process quality problems should be traced back to source and corrected. Guidance on process audits is given in each of the IT Infrastructure Library modules and a general approach to process auditing is described in the IT Infrastructure Library **Quality Audit** module. The use by the FM provider of IT Infrastructure Library principles and practices is recommended as a sound basis for running a quality IT service.

5.2.3 Service, applications and usage plans

Service review meetings will from time to time take a forward look at usage plans. The successful operation of an FM contract requires that the FM provider is aware, sufficiently far in advance, of planned changes in the pattern of IT service usage so as to propose and implement changes to accommodate them. The IT Infrastructure Library **Capacity Management** module gives advice on this subject.

5.3 People

5.3.1 Service Control Team

The SCT needs to maintain up to date knowledge of the technology available, and of that being used by the FM provider. The SCT also has ongoing responsibility for monitoring the quality of service provision and for auditing the processes used to provide it. The SCT is responsible for representing the users' interests with the FM provider on all aspects of IT service provision.

5.4 Timing

The SCT requires management reports from the FM provider at regular intervals (probably weekly). The information therein is used as briefing material for the monthly service review meetings.

Quarterly the organization should take a longer term view of the service provided and a forward look at planned usage, and should audit the FM provider's processes.

Annually there should be an independent review of all aspects of IT service provision, including the efficiency and effectiveness of the FM provider and of the SCT, and where necessary changes should be instigated by senior management without delay. Workload and usage plans should be reviewed annually. These reviews are input to the organization's annual review of IS strategy. Tactical plans are formulated to coincide with the organization's annual budget-setting, to cover resource requirements for the following Financial Year.

6. Benefits, Costs and Possible Problems

This section covers the benefits, costs and possible problems of both moving to FM and of managing it in accordance with the guidance contained in earlier sections.

In essence, if an organization follows the guidance given in this module it can be sure of managing FM to provide quality IT services. There is an investment cost, but the organization can have confidence that its requirements will be met consistently and that it will not become locked into a particular FM company.

6.1 Benefits

Putting their IT service provision out to FM allows organizations to concentrate on their mainstream business. However, organizations must manage their relationships with an FM provider to have confidence that quality IT services - needed to support the efficient and effective running of their businesses - will be provided. The guidance given in this module assists organizations to manage their relationships with FM providers.

6.1.1 The Business-like approach

The principles and practices described in the IT Infrastructure Library help organizations to carry out the management of their IT infrastructures and to provide IT services to support their businesses in a business-like manner - cost-effectively and aligned to customer needs. Using this guidance to manage FM can help engender a more business-like approach internally to the provision of IT services, as well as formalizing the service provision contractually.

This business-like approach to IT service provision is based on:

* a specification of user requirements in SLAs

* a structured approach to reviewing users' SLRs and coping with changes to them

* a structured approach to monitoring the quality of IT service provision against the SLAs

* effective change and problem management systems, as recommended by the IT Infrastructure Library modules, to handle deficiencies in service quality and changes in requirements.

6.1.2 Skill Shortage

The use of an FM provider reduces the burden of recruitment, training and retention of scarce IT personnel.

6.1.3 Cost Savings

Savings can often be achieved by the FM provider sharing out the cost of resources such as accommodation, hardware, expert staff and networks, among several customers, although some of these savings may be offset by higher staff costs. Some FM providers quote savings on the customer's IT budget of up to 25% from using FM. However, if organizations have less common equipment or requirements, impose heavy constraints or are already using their existing facilities very efficiently, they may find that there are little, if any, savings.

6.1.4 Accountability

A significant benefit of passing responsibility for IT services on to an FM provider is that the FM provider then becomes the prime contractor, responsible for the resolution of any problems with other suppliers (eg hardware or networks). If SLAs are not being met, the burden of day to day responsibility lies with the prime contractor.

Many IT Directorates in customer organizations are having great difficulty in providing the services being demanded by their users and meeting the required timescales. One way of meeting these requirements may be by FM supplying a distinct part of the service, particularly in an area where a detailed knowledge of the business issues is not required. This is often a better solution than spreading the existing computer expertise and backing it up with consultants. Giving the FM provider responsibility for a distinct part of the service also increases the accountability of the external staff, by making it easier to define and measure their responsibilities.

6.1.5 Regulating Costs

Although there is no reason why costs cannot be regulated when the service is being provided internally, experience shows that, at present, they are less likely to be calculated or adhered to as stringently. A benefit that FM can provide is the ability to regulate IT costs better. This has the obvious advantage of allowing accurate forecasting of expenditure to be done more easily. Typically a predetermined monthly/quarterly/yearly payment is made, sometimes with a usage element on top. (This pre-determined payment will be adjusted annually by means of an index linked variation formula using appropriate published indices). If the FM service was being provided on a 'bureau' or 'tariff' basis, with charges based solely on the amount of resource used, it would not be so easy to predetermine costs - although still perhaps slightly easier to regulate them than for internal IT service provision.

6.1.6 Reducing Staff Levels

Another possible advantage is the ability to reduce the organization's staff numbers. Devolving responsibility for a distinct part (eg operations) or all of IT service provision may be a way to maintain service levels, while reducing the staff numbers. Alternatively, existing human resources could be released for use elsewhere in the organization. This could include managerial as well as technical expertise.

6.1.7 Adding Expertise and Resources

FM providers have, in many cases, greater IT expertise and resources (human and physical) particularly compared to some organizations with smaller or more embryonic IT sections. Even when organizations have large numbers of people, they can still be affected by skill shortages. An FM provider contracts to provide a service and has to cope with any resultant expertise or resource problems.

6.1.8 Development Time

If it is accepted that greater human and physical resources are likely to be available to FM providers, it is reasonable to assume that the time taken for an FM provider to develop systems may compare favourably with that for an internal IT Directorate.

6.1.9 Alternative Solutions

In the course of taking over an existing IT service, an FM provider may be able to see an alternative method of providing such a service. This alternative may not be immediately obvious to the existing internal IT section, which may be deeply immersed in existing practices.

6.2 Costs

It is in an organization's best interest that the company providing its FM is business-like and profit-making. This means, however, that the more demanding the requirement (eg faster transaction response times, sole use of hardware etc), the greater the cost is likely to be.

Organizations should ensure the costs they incur to run particular workloads accurately reflect the needs and priorities of their various businesses. This is primarily a matter of satisfactorily specifying service level, and other requirements.

6.2.1 Comparing different providers' charges

As stated in 6.1.3, FM providers can in some circumstances supply a service more cheaply than an in-house provider. Only detailed analysis of particular requirements can decide whether FM is cheaper. Organizations should note that the current costs for IT services are not always clearly identifiable (eg computer stationery and electrical power costs may not be included in the IT budget), and furthermore the services may not be provided to the scope and service levels specified in an SSR for FM. However, if the organization already uses IT Infrastructure Library principles and practices, and all prospective FM providers of the service agree to do the same, the user can more easily compare costs as well as being sure that quality processes are being used.

6.2.2 Location of hardware

Consider where the hardware should be sited. Some organizations may find it financially beneficial to site their hardware with the FM provider, and so allow shared use with other customers, (although the organization might still retain ownership). In deciding whether to ask for hardware to be located on site, consider:

*   how lightly the system is loaded

*   how standard and stable the requirement is

*   whether there are any exceptional security requirements.

6.2.3 Set-up charges

Any initial outlay by the FM provider can be recovered as a set-up charge or can be spread across the periodic payments which are made for the provision of the service.

6.2.4 Method of charging

Periodic payments can be made at any set interval (monthly, quarterly, yearly) and are generally at a predetermined cost. This cost is normally increased annually by means of an index linked variation formula using appropriate published indices. If FM is being provided on a bureau basis, and in certain other circumstances, the charge can be based on actual resources used (eg human, machine time, materials). This method will make budgeting more difficult as the cost could vary greatly from one interval to the next.

6.2.5 Cost of change

All changes, if they require implementation or operational costs above an agreed threshold, will be charged. To satisfy itself that reasonable charges are being made for changes the organizations can compare rates for different FM providers. The SCT and the teams carrying out the annual independent reviews of the FM service can be asked to examine the FM provider's charges and judge whether they are reasonable - particularly the charges for changes. To guard against complacency by the FM provider the organization can instigate periodic termination and renewal points in the contract.

6.2.6 Cost of Managing FM

A number of costs are incurred for work associated with adequately managing FM. These cover:

* planning for FM including activities associated with production and agreement of a contract

* the setting up and maintaining of an SCT

* start-up and hand-over costs

* any conversion or transfer costs

* ongoing costs of monitoring the quality of IT service and the FM provider's performance, and any follow-up action

* ongoing cost of planning (and implementing changes - see 6.2.5), to meet future requirements

* costs of auditing the FM provider's activities and of the independent external audits/reviews, and any follow-up action.

6.3 Possible Problems

6.3.1 Dependence on FM Provider

Once an organization hands over its IT provision to an FM provider there is genuine concern that it can become locked into one provider.

To counter this, include in the contract predetermined handover procedures which allow another party to take over from the FM provider. This increases control and reduces the risk of becoming locked into the particular provider.

As an added safeguard the organization must ensure that agreed processes are followed, and agreed standards are adhered to, by the FM provider.

CCTA recommends that organizations require FM providers to supply their service according to IT Infrastructure Library principles and practices and that their IT infrastructure management processes should be quality certified to ISO 9001.

6.3.2 Lack of Flexibility

Organizations are bound to be concerned about how much flexibility they have with an FM provider. Once a contract is signed for a particular service to be provided what happens when senior management require a change of direction?

Arrangements for change should be incorporated in the contract. Sufficient flexibility should be allowed to enable the FM provider to cope if the organization's business objectives change.

6.3.3 Cost of Change

The organization may find a large price being demanded when its requirements change. In general users need to know they are not being overcharged for amendments (see 6.2.5).

Consider renewing the contract annually, say after the first 2 years, to help ensure charges are competitive. (The administrative overhead may well quickly 'pay for itself' in cash savings or in improved service). Ensuring the contract contains a method for costing changes (eg fixed hourly rate for change building and ongoing service cost - both index linked) also helps to control the cost of change.

Many change types are foreseeable, such as changes to:

* workload volumes

* service levels

* the scope of the service.

The basis for costing such changes can be built into the original contract.

6.3.4 Staff and Trade Union Side Reaction

An important factor for management to consider when looking at FM is the staff and Trade Union (TU) side's reaction. The attitude may vary depending on whether an existing service is being transferred to FM, or FM is being used to provide a new service. The reaction of staff, in both cases, is likely to be based on how their conditions of service are affected.

If the FM provider is to provide a new service, the major staff problem could be one of morale: existing staff may see themselves as being left with the more mundane jobs. This could well exacerbate some of the problems which first made the FM contract attractive (eg skills shortage).

If it can be demonstrated that a new service cannot easily be provided without using consultancy or FM there may be more favourable reaction from the TUs and their members.

6.3.5 Loss of Expertise

A problem that is particularly difficult for many organizations to overcome is the loss of expertise. It is already evident that some organizations have problems holding on to their skilled staff, especially in the South East and the major cities. It is therefore very unlikely that such organizations would be able to attract IT staff in sufficient numbers to rebuild their IT expertise, if that proved necessary, once they have transferred to FM. A possible exception is if a large organization transferred a small part of its IT services to FM.

However, organizations can maintain and foster some internal IT expertise in their Service Control Teams. This may facilitate a return to in-house provision of IT services, if expertise can be heavily supplemented by short-term consultancy and contract staff.

The SCT may itself suffer from wastage. Fill any vacancies as quickly as possible with IT literate people and ensure they are given all necessary training.

6.3.6 Production of the Statement of Service Requirement and Contract

Many customer organizations have experience in producing Operational Requirements for hardware and/or software. However, few have been through an FM procurement cycle. Government organizations can obtain advice from CCTA or from the CCTA IS Guide on Facilities Management.

6.3.7 Quality Audit

When IT services are provided internally, it is normal practice to have an independent quality audit function within the IT Directorate. When IT service is provided by an FM provider, a quality audit function run by the FM provider could not guarantee to represent the organization's interests. (The FM provider can of course run an internal quality audit function for its own purposes.) Make it a condition of the contract that the SCT acts as a quality audit function, independent of the FM provider.

6.3.8 FM Provider Unwilling to Use IT Infrastructure Library

A problem may arise if an FM provider resists the use of IT Infrastructure Library principles and practices. Organizations should counter this by explaining the benefits. Most FM providers, if well organized, are already using practices that are not very far removed from IT Infrastructure Library ones.

7. Tools

Tools are necessary to manage the IT infrastructure and therefore to manage the FM provider. It would not be possible, for instance, adequately to monitor levels of service provision without tools.

Which tools are required varies depending on how much of the IT service and of the IT infrastructure management activity is passed to FM (see figure 2, page 9). Details of the tools required for the various parts of IT infrastructure management are included in section 7 of each of the other IT Infrastructure Library modules.

All IT infrastructure management tools and related data must be available for inspection and use under predetermined conditions by the SCT. Special arrangements are necessary if use of the tools could have an impact on the service. However, the SCT should be given unlimited access to monitoring tools wherever possible.

If the FM provider plans to introduce either a new tool or a new release of an existing tool, especially one concerned with IT planning or service quality monitoring, the organization must be informed as a condition of the contract. This enables the organization to evaluate the functionality of the tool and the information it produces to ensure it is acceptable or, if it is not, to discuss with the FM provider the changes required to make it acceptable.

Annex A. Glossary of Terms

Acronyms and abbreviations used in this module

CCTA	Central Computer and Telecommunications Agency
CRAMM	CCTA Risk Analysis and Management Method
FM	Facilities Management
IS	Information Systems
IT	Information Technology
NACCB	National Accreditation Council for Certification Bodies
PRINCE	Projects in Controlled Environments
SCT	Service Control Team
SLA	Service Level Agreement
SLR	Service Level Requirement
SSADM	Structured Systems Analysis and Design Method
SSR	Statement of Service Requirement
TU	Trades Union.

Definitions

Availability	The proportion of time that the service is actually available for use by the user, within the agreed service times. This is calculated as follows: % Availability = (Available Time/ Agreed Service Time) x 100 [eg the service is available for 39 hours within a 40 hour agreed service time period: (39/ 40) x 100 = 97.5% availability]. NB. A service may be available to one or more users at the same time that it is unavailable to others, due to component failure. Each user will therefore have his/her own perception of availability.
Back Out	Procedures necessary to cancel or postpone the project and either return to the status quo or implement a contingency plan.

CC88	CCTA Rules for tendering and general conditions of contract covering supply and services for information technology and private branch exchange systems.
Environmental Infrastructure	The building, cabling/services facilities, and furnishings to support the physical needs of IT and users.
Facilities Management	The provision of the management, and operation and support of an organization's computers and/or networks by an external source at agreed service levels. The service will generally be provided for a set time at agreed cost.
Hand-over	The period during which an organization hands over the running of part or all of its IT service provision to an FM provider, or when an FM provider is relinquishing the contract to another provider at the end of the contract.
ISO 9001	An international quality management and quality assurance standard for use when conformance to specified requirements is to be assured by the provider during several stages which may include design/development, production, installation and servicing.
Key Personnel	Skilled personnel (usually on the FM Provider's staff) involved in the provision of the IT service.
Nominated FM Manager	The representative of the FM provider responsible for liaising with the customer organization (usually the organization's SCT).
PRINCE	(enhanced version of PROMPT) - The method adopted within government for planning, managing and controlling IS projects. It provides guidance on the management components (organization, plans and controls) and on the technical components (end products and the activities needed to produce them).
Service Charge Credit	A credit given against the normal service charge, normally used when service quality, or the FM provider's performance, falls below any thresholds agreed in the contract.
Service Control Team	A team of people with skills roughly equivalent to business analysts who will be responsible for managing an FM provider on behalf of the user organization.

Service Level Agreement	A written agreement or 'contract' between the users and the IT service provider which documents the agreed service levels for an IT service. Typically it will cover: service hours, service availability, user support levels, throughputs and terminal response times, restrictions, functionality and the service levels to be provided in a contingency. It may also include security and accounting policy.
Service Level Requirement	A statement of service levels required by a user (see also Service Level Agreement).
Start-up	The period at the start of the contract during which the new FM provider takes over the provision of IT service.
Tempest	The shielding of Electronic Information Processing (EIP) equipment to protect against the leakage of information caused by the emanation of radiation through, for example, free space, telecommunications lines and power lines.

Annex B. Guidance on Key Service Items and Quantifying Functionality

Guidance on Key Service Items to be Monitored

It is recommended that the following items be monitored (they are of equal relevance to both centralized and distributed systems):

1. Availability and Reliability

* the achieved overall service availability within contracted service hours

* the achieved overall service availability within total service hours (this includes contracted hours, plus any extensions)

* terminal availability (where relevant). This can be monitored at individual terminal level or a formula such as that shown below can be used to produce a single figure giving a broad idea of overall terminal availability.

$$\frac{(\text{No.VDUs} \times \text{total mins sched.}) - \text{sum of (No.VDUs} \times \text{mins down})}{\text{No.VDUs} \times \text{total mins sched.}} \times 100$$

* the number of service failures

* the amount of downtime per failure

* the number of jobs that have to be re-run due to error.

2. Performance

* Response times

* batch turnaround times

* throughput rates.

Monitoring tools used must be set-up to produce reports reflecting the user/agreement structure to reduce the amount of manual effort involved.

3. Functionality

The functionality of all service aspects must be monitored. See below for guidance on quantifying functionality. All fault reporting mechanisms must include provision for recording levels of severity. .

4. Printing/Paper Handling

Records must be kept of all printed output produced and any paper handling work carried out. This will be particularly important where charging algorithms include this effort.

5. Accounting

All IT resources used must be monitored and accounted for, to allow for charging or notional charging. This also provides valuable management information allowing more efficient resource usage.

Guidance on Quantifying Functionality

Regardless of how rigorous Quality Assurance and Testing procedures are, no significant IT system will ever be completely error free. Whenever errors are detected it is important to assess the severity in order to decide what priority and resources, if any, should be allocated to resolving the problem.

All Service Level Agreements must include some agreed minimum level of acceptable functional requirement. In order to achieve this in a quantifiable way some form of severity rating scale must be agreed, resulting in all errors being given a severity 'score'. In the suggested scale shown below the range is 0 to 9, with 9 being most severe. The SLA should include the agreed acceptable number of errors that can be tolerated at each level during the reporting period. All fault reporting mechanisms must include provision for severity levels to be recorded, and these must be monitored, and comparisons must be made with the SLAs.

Suggested Rating Scale

In descending level of severity:

9 Gives wrong results, but no one discovers it right away. By the time it is discovered, there is no way to undo the damage. Issuing duplicate cheques might be an example of this error.

8 Destroys a lot of data, with no way to recover.

7 a Destroys data, but can be recovered or re-entered with considerable effort

    b A legislative change fails to work at all

    c Service crashes and the user does not recover within the time period the user would normally expect (needs to be agreed and specified).

6 a A feature which used to work, and on which the user has come to depend, fails to work at all

    b The service fails, but it recovers in a normal period of time.

5 A new feature fails to work, but no one is yet dependent on it.

4 A feature is usable, but works differently from how the specification said it would, leading to some difficulty in its use.

3 A message to the public contains some major spelling errors, but it is understandable.

2 A message to the user contains some major spelling errors, but it is understandable.

1 A message to the (internal) operator contains some major spelling error, but the message is understandable.

0 There is a very minor difference between the specification and what was developed, but everyone could live with the error indefinitely. For example a spelling error in a message that no one had ever seen displayed.

Note ! - Any errors not specifically covered on the list must be equated in terms of severity and a 'score' allocated.

Annex C. Skeleton Service Level Agreement

The following document is a skeleton SLA upon which organizations can model their own agreements.This model will also be used as a basis for support tools and training courses which CCTA will be developing in the future. It is therefore recommended that organizations that may wish to use these facilities should use this standard format for their own agreements.

The figures included in the skeleton agreement are examples only and must not be regarded as definitive guidance.

Skeleton Service Level Agreement

This Service Level Agreement is between _____

and SCT on behalf of_____ .

The agreement is for the provision of the _____

_____

transaction processing service and associated batch processing, as detailed in later
paragraphs.

This agreement remains valid until superseded by a revised agreement mutually endorsed by
the signatories below. It will be reviewed on a six-monthly basis. Minor changes to the
agreement may be recorded on the form at the end of the agreement providing, once again,
they are mutually endorsed by the two parties.

Service:_____TP Service	Start Date dd/mm/yy
Service Manager: A.N.Other	Renewal Date dd/mm/yy

Signatories

Name	Date	Title
A.N.Other	dd/mm/yy	IT Services Manager
A.N.Other	dd/mm/yy	_____Branch Manager

Dates of previous amendments:

_____ _____ _____ _____ _____ _____ _____

_____ _____ _____ _____ _____ .

Service Description

The _____ Transaction Processing service has the following functions:

_____

_____

_____

The applications running under this service are as follows:

_____   _____

_____   _____

_____   _____

The major transaction types are:

Identity	Description
_____	_____
_____	_____
_____	_____
_____	_____

Service Hours

The service is normally available as follows:

Mon to Thurs-	**08:00hrs to 18:00hrs**
Fri-	**08:00hrs to 16:30hrs**

Special conditions for weekends and bank holidays are as follows:

_____ .

Pre-scheduled maintenance/housekeeping is carried out on the first Tuesday in every month

but should not impact on the _____ TP service.

The procedures to be followed for requesting changes to the service hours are:

    Temporary changes/extensions;_____

    _____ .

    Permanent changes;_____

    _____ .

Service Availability

The minimum percentage availability during normal service hours for any user of this service is **96%**. The average percentage availability for all users is **98%**.

The maximum number of service breaks to be tolerated per rolling 4 week period is **3**.

The maximum time to recover from a service break is **35** mins.

The maximum percentages of batch jobs that have to be re-run due to error are:

    Total- **6%**.

    Excluding incorrect submissions- **3%**.

The measurement period is a rolling 4 week period.

Details of special conditions are as follows: _____

_____ .

User support Levels

All problems, queries or requests for assistance must be made to the user Help Desk on Ext. **123**. The Help Desk will be manned from **07:30 to 18:00** each week-day.

Normally calls to the Help Desk must be made only by group liaison officers or their deputies.

Where a problem cannot be immediately resolved the Help Desk staff channel it to the appropriate technical support area. The caller is advised by the Help Desk as soon as a solution is found, or kept informed of progress where appropriate.

Target fault resolution times are as follows:

Severity Level	Times (Hrs)
9	1
8	1
7	1
6	2
5	4
4	8
3	24
2	48
1	at next release
0	at next release

User guide distribution and updating details are as follows_____

_____ .

Annex D. Items to be considered for inclusion in draft contracts

This annex is based on a subsection of the CCTA IS Guide on Procurement. Further details and guidance are available from CCTA Procurement Division.

D1 Main Clauses

The following points for inclusion in the main clauses of a draft contract should be considered by an organization during the procurement stage of an FM contract:

* duration of contract

* termination rights

* assistance on termination/handover

* limitation of liability

* force majeure

* audit access

* Intellectual Property Rights(IPR)

* indemnities

* warranties

* entire agreement.

The questions to be raised against the above points are now detailed.

D1.1 Duration of contract

How long should the contract last?

Does the organization commit to the same period as the provider or to a shorter period?

Does the contract provide for extension after an initial period?

D1.2 Termination rights

What termination rights should the organization have?

If the organization has to terminate what further rights should accrue; for example should the organization plan to have the right, on termination, to purchase equipment owned by the provider and to obtain assignment of licences?

D1.3 Assistance on termination/handover

How should an organization plan for changes of provider?

What level of assistance from the existing provider should be sought on handover to a new provider?

How should such assistance be specified within the contract?

D1.4 Limitation of liability

Should a provider assume unlimited liability for economic loss?

If not, can an organization assess easily what its financial losses might be in the event of provider default?

To what extent should "consequential loss" exclusion clauses be admitted?

Should there be damages at large or liquidated damages?

Should any agreement on limitation of liability be reciprocal?

D1.5 Force majeure

To what extent should both parties be relieved from responsibility for events supposedly beyond their control, for example should industrial dispute be admitted as a force majeure circumstance?

What protection, if any, should be given to a prime provider who is reliant on a number of other contractors and suppliers for delivery of the service?

D1.6 Audit access

What provision should an organization make for an audit of the processes and of the IT infrastructure?

How often should audits be done and who should undertake them (the organization or an independent third party)?

D1.7 Intellectual Property Rights (IPR)

Should the organization retain IPR over any software that is commissioned by it and/or maintained/developed by the provider?

If so, what specific form of ownership should the organization stipulate (eg should government bodies stipulate that software will be Crown Copyright)?

D1.8 Indemnities

What protection is necessary against third party claims in respect of alleged infringements of third party rights, for example patents, copyright, other IPR?

Usual practice is for the FM provider to indemnify the organization against such claims.

This is important because the FM provider normally has so much responsibility for and control over the environment supporting the service.

D1.9 Warranties

Should the organization seek particular types of warranty as a means of emphasizing to the provider its responsibilities for providing quality IT services, or are there sufficient commitments built into the contract schedules to safeguard organizational interests?

D1.10 Entire Agreement

Has consideration been given to insertion of an 'entire agreement' clause? (such a clause, which is intended to mean that the contract supersedes all prior agreements, may well be a useful discipline on the basis that agreement between the parties is expressed in precise terms, in one place and is not concealed in subsidiary documents. However, despite an entire agreement clause, pre-contract documents may still be enforceable, for example under the Misrepresentation Acts).

D2 Schedules

Schedules particularly, because they describe operations and administration, vary considerably from contract to contract. The following schedules are almost certainly required, however.

D2.1 Descriptions of Services

Such a schedule (or numbers of schedules) is fundamental to the contract. What is the provider to deliver by way of services?

The schedules are constructed from requirement and proposed solution and identify all those aspects of a provider's offering which are to be provided, including Service Levels/Agreements and supporting activity such as:

* liaison

* standards and conformance

* testing

* project control

* Help Desk

* problem management

* change management

* help on handover

* operations management

* configuration management/software control

* capacity management/growth

* security management

* availability management

* service level management

* accommodation

* training and education.

It is in these areas that an organization must be able to understand and audit the procedures as well as the results.

D2.2 Timetable

When is the organization getting the FM service? Are there to be phases in the provision of that service?

D2.3 Acceptance

How does the organization accept the service, including interim acceptance on a phased basis?

D2.4 FM provider's performance against contract

How does the organization monitor and measure ongoing service levels after acceptance? How does the organization use contractual sanctions to help ensure that the necessary service levels are met?

D2.5 Charges

How does the organization pay and what is the structure of the charges?

D2.6 Variation of Charges

How does the organization regulate what is paid in future years? Does the contract vary charges annually, more frequently, less frequently, or not at all? What is the mechanism - index-linking or something else?

D2.7 Invoicing

What is the frequency of payment and what is the billing system?

D2.8 Audit of Service

The organization must consider three types of audit:

* that discharging any statutory or accounting obligations

* that looking at the processes used

* that looking at the quality of the service provided (usually called monitoring - see above).

D2.9 Change Control

An FM contract requires clearly defined principles and procedures governing the inevitable need to introduce change.

D2.10 Authority Obligations

There are two parties to the contract and the organization may recognize the advantages of identifying precisely, and recording as a schedule, its own obligations.

IT Infrastructure Library
Managing Facilities Management   Comments Sheet

CCTA hopes that you find this book both useful and interesting. We will welcome your
comments and suggestions for improving it.
Please use this form or a photocopy, and continue on a further sheet if needed.

From: re: 1990/MFM
        Name

    Organization

      Address

    Telephone

COVERAGE
Does the material cover your needs?
If not, then what additional material would you like included.

CLARITY
Are there any points which are unclear?
If yes, please detail where and why.

ACCURACY
Please give details of any inaccuracies found.

If more space is required for these or other comments, please continue overleaf.

OTHER COMMENTS

Return to: **IT Infrastructure Management Services**
Central Computer and Telecommunications Agency
Gildengate House
Upper Green Lane
NORWICH, NR3 1DW

Further information

Further information on the contents of this module can be obtained from:

IT Infrastructure Management Services
CCTA
Gildengate House
Upper Green Lane
NORWICH
NR3 1DW

Telephone 0603 694788
(GTN 3014 - 4788).

Printed in the United Kingdom for HMSO
Dd289144 4/90 C10 G3390 10170